How God Does Sustainability

A set of thoughts for every day of the Year

Tim Daniel

© 2025 Timothy Daniel
All rights reserved.
NO AI TRAINING
ISBN 9798218868512
Library of Congress Control Number: 2025924521
Cover photo by Mason Field on Unsplash
First Edition 2025

Acknowledgments

To the lady at the concert, who somehow knew God was not done with me after all.

Prologue

There are intractable problems that have always bedeviled human civilizations, leaving open questions and festering wounds.

We have been unable to create widespread, inclusive, and lasting happiness.

We have been unable to build change processes into our social arrangements, so that we keep adapting to what is going on around us to create something better for everyone.

We have been unable to live together peacefully while remaining different from each other.

We have been unable to build civilizations that endure and thrive as a healthy, natural part of earth.

In nature we see something very different.

We see spontaneous playfulness. Even with the ever-present threat of disease, injury or attack, creatures somehow find ways to enjoy themselves. We see constant innovation and extravagant beauty. We see complex, highly diverse communities of life, living alongside each other. We find evidence that life has endured, despite everything thrown at it, and that life is overcoming its current threats right now in surprising ways.

Clearly, our Creator has embedded in creation a way of solving problems that we lack no longer have access to. To create sustainability, we must re-learn God's way of solving the problems that arise from sharing one small planet. Unsustainable civilizations are the culmination of human efforts to solve these problems apart from God and nature. After such civilizations collapse we must figure out how to survive. But the key question is - to survive as what?

As a people who make better choices for better reasons.

To evolve into such a people, we must be realistic about our starting point. Currently those of us who seek God live as a conquered and occupied people. In sympathy with all nature, we groan under the rule of a stupid, wasteful and unjust system, one opposed with all its might to the rule of God on earth, and one that is actively at war with earth's living systems.

Yet we do not despair, resign or wallow in self-pity. Instead, we work daily, under the radar, preparing for the day we will break out, spread out, and start building. Under God's daily direction, we will create something new and natural. We will be the founders of a society designed to participate in life, on life's terms, for as long as there is life on earth.

God is not done with us. Over the course of the next year, we will unpack the essential components of a godly civilization that will endure long enough to do what God needs done.

To track our progress, we will use the same system used at large manufacturing facilities, where one sees a board showing the number of days since the last accident. Our goal will be to get through 365 days without injury, which is impossible to do under the rule of the godless.

Day 1

We are part of the earth; we are not apart from the earth.

Life on earth will go on with or without humanity. The opposite cannot be said.

We are here for the earth, and the earth is here for us. We need each other because we sustain and complete each other. The earth's open-ended, unfinished completeness explains why we exist, as we are essential to bring it about by using creative capacities no other species possesses.

We are here to help. As long as we accept that, God will help us. God will meet our real needs, so we can fulfill the function intended for us, but will not help us when we intend to do anything else with our unique human faculties.

Day 2

The earth belongs to God; the earth does not belong to us.

The earth's potential future creations also belong to God. We can't know what that future looks like, but from studying what God has created in nature, we know it will be characterized by extravagant and ever-growing diversity. There will be harmony and happiness, but a harmony and happiness that is different than we have pursued before.

Up until now we thought harmony must mean being alike and agreeing on everything.

Up until now we thought happiness must mean all pleasure and no pain.

Those thoughts were lies that led us inevitably to build unsustainable and ultimately violent civilizations.

Day 3

In the future, God has in store for earth wonderful things that have always been possible but have not yet come together. They are possible because by using a constant flow of new information from God, we can use everything we find lying around us and inside us and between us, and everything we experience, to construct a surprising, higher way of living.

Everything we need to start the work is already here, available, and accessible to all, everywhere always. At first it does not appear to be a lot, but we find it is always enough to begin and do the next thing each day. That's all we need anyway.

Day 4

As with all other living things, among us there will continue to be pain and loss, but there will be much less suffering – which is the fear of future pain and loss. Pain and loss are found in our real, observable, measurable circumstances. Therefore, it is only in our circumstances that we can find real, observable, testable, measurable means to avoid, minimize and recover from pain and loss.

Suffering is found in our imagination, reacting to things that are not observable, measurable, and testable. In our imagination we find no real, testable, improvable means to avoid, minimize, or recover from our imaginary pain. When we are chased by ghosts there is nothing that will make them stop chasing us.

Day 5

To hallucinate is to see something that is not there. To have a blind spot is to not see something that is there, often the single most important variable in a situation.

Neither God, nor nature, nor our group will meet us and live with us in our hallucinations. So we live in constant touch with God, with nature and with each other in small, cooperative problem-solving groups.

We don't live in our heads. Hallucinations cause blind spots. So we take pains to face the facts of our real shared situation. We don't seek escape. We seek relevant and useful contact with reality, starting with the ultimate reality – our Creator. We learn what does and does not work by staying in constant contact with what embodies the genius of God – nature.

Day 6

Since we seek and live in the presence of God daily, and since God is the God of reality, we live in and respond effectively to our actual, often mess and confusing situation. We are not chased by ghosts, and we do not chase ghosts.

It is in reality, and in reality alone that God meets, teaches, and helps us. And it is there we find, usually within 24 hours, when we cry out to God, and turn to each other, that we are provided with whatever it is we need to meet the real challenges of the day. Usually, we can make a small adjustment to what we are doing with what we already have in hand, and it is enough to deal with the day's concern.

Day 7

Even though we experience real pain and loss, we often experience hours of creative play.

Since we are helpful and cooperative, going through pain and loss together significantly reduces how long it lasts and how bad it is. We do not seek to eliminate all pain and suffering, as it is our own pain and suffering that teaches us empathy. As a result, we feel compassion for those who are hurting, and we know they too probably fear the pain they could face in the future.

Since we treat each other with empathy and kindness during painful times, those who are new to our company come to realize they don't have to fret over being betrayed, abandoned, or attacked by us in addition to bearing the pain itself.

When we are in peril, we don't need to waste precious energy imagining all the terrible things that might happen to us that haven't yet happened to us.

Instead, drawing comfort and strength from God's presence and the support we provide for each other, all we need to do is look at the facts of our actual situation today.

Day 8

When making our way through a time of pain or danger we learn to pay attention to what is right here, right now. We find something we can work with to protect and provide for ourselves and for those in our care.

Since we don't need to waste energy protecting ourselves from each other, we can put that energy toward recovery from any pain or loss may experience.

It is recovery from pain and loss that makes us truly value well-being. Before pain, loss, and recovery, we took well-being for granted and even felt entitled to it.

Walking alongside each other through cycles of pain, loss, and recovery, we become an ever more grateful, careful, competent, and compassionate people.

The experience motivates us to build systems that make loss less likely to happen in the first place and recovery more likely when it does happen.

We are careful to make sure our new systems don't cause loss for other people or other creatures.

Day 9

For us there is a balance between work and rest. Our work is meaningful, interesting, and varied, so it is not soul-crushing. We get tired *in* what we do for a living, but we can recover by resting in the safety we provide for each other.

We do not get tired *of* what we do for a living, because we help each other find and do what each of us was created by God to do.

Our way of living is accessible to everyone and at a cost anyone can pay. The cost of participation is the best each of us can contribute using our time, attention, energy, and God-given talents. We practice including anyone and everyone who earns a place by giving the best they have, no matter who they are or where they come from.

Day 10

In a sustainable future we will be alive to nature. Nature will speak to us and teach us. In nature we see tension and mutual opposition between different groups and species, but in a healthy ecosystem we don't see one type of life eradicating another type of life.

Sustainability itself must be sustainable. It takes ongoing social organization for a society to live in sustainable ways. To date, sustainability efforts, though technically brilliant, lacked sufficient social organization to continue without massive external intervention and subsidy. As soon as the subsidies stopped so did the brilliant sustainability efforts. Something was missing.

Sustainability is the way we relate to our environment sustained by the way we relate to each other. The way we relate to each other is a natural outgrowth from how we relate to the One who created us and our environment. That is the same One who made us different from each other.

Day 11

God delights in diversity. We are not the same. We do not agree on everything. This is no mistake. There will be natural tension and opposition between us just as the beams of vaulted ceiling push equally against each other, creating a stable structure and a protected living space below.

Our relationship with God limits what we will do to oppose each other. We limit each other without eliminating each other. Natural forces, when unleashed and unlimited, tear apart complex systems. Natural forces kept within natural limits harness those same forces to produce dynamic systems capable of constant adaptive change.

Accepting the existence of another life but only if it eliminates its differences to become a copy of ourselves is just another form of genocide. Among us, neither side will attempt to eliminate or convert the other, as each realizes it needs the other to exist as it is - just as much as it needs to exist itself, as it is.

Day 12

We need those who oppose us with equal strength because they limit our excesses, and we limit theirs. They push us to act when we would otherwise be too passive, and we do the same to them.

Those who oppose us are usually more keenly aware of our errors than we are, and we are more keenly aware of their errors than they are.

When we try to prove their critique of our ways wrong, we find out they are on to something. Now we must either correct our errors or give up any claim to integrity. The same happens to them. Both of us grow to be more functional and honest.

Day 13

We exist to assist the Creator in the on-going work of creation. We must remain fluid, flexible, attentive, and responsive to be of any use to God. So long as we stay in this fully available state of mind, we can fulfill our function and remain a vital part of the earth, in some form.

We have no right to do anything that prevents anything life could still do on earth. Instead, our role and responsibility is to do anything and everything God requires each day, right where we are, to help earth do what it can still do but has not yet done.

Life as we know it on earth is exceedingly rare in the universe. Earth can support complex life and currently, we know of no other place in the universe that can. In fact, there is a very strong logical argument that there is no other place in the universe that can.

The Creator will not allow one species to destroy something so rare and valuable. God will stop the destruction, using the natural consequence of our own choices as a civilization.

Day 14

God will take back the earth, just as surely as the sun always emerges again after a total eclipse.

Life comes pre-loaded with infinite new possibilities that have not yet become realities. The question isn't whether God will intervene to protect the full unrealized potential of life on earth.

The only open question for us is whose side we will be on as God moves to reclaim control over the earth, to restore humanity's natural role in its unfolding story.

This book is for those who have already chosen to stay on God's side in the struggle, and to stay close by God's side through whatever happens along the way. We are those who will remain.

Day 15

Water comes in three forms: liquid, gas (steam), and solid (ice). In its liquid form water can go places and do things it can't do in its other forms. The transition from one form to another is called a critical point, a phase transition.

Two units of water in the same form or phase can merge and form a greater unit with potentially greater force. A unit of water and one of ice or steam can't do this. Being in the same phase, at the same time, at the same place, is essential if something new and different is going to happen.

Two minds in different phases can't interact in any productive way and will often block or counteract each other. If we are out of sync, out of phase with God and creation, we are not only useless, but destructive. If we stay in sync, in phase with God and creation we are useful and productive.

Day 16

Those who refuse to seek God's direction and correction are out of phase, out of sync, and are being phased out of earth's future.

Those who constantly seek God's direction, inspection and correction come to live in sync with God and are being phased into earth's future. To be in the same phase as someone else is to see what they see when they see it, the way they see it, and to respond in a way that makes sense to them. To be out of phase is to not see that another sees, not hear what they hear, not feel what they feel, and not respond in a way that is helpful and useful to them.

To be in the same phase of creation as God is to know God's goals. To be in sync with God means to know from experience how God accomplishes those goals, and to constantly build a life that allows us to be helpful and useful all the way through whatever happens along the way.

Day 17

To stay in the same phase of creation as God, we are open, not closed. We receive input from our environment and add social value to it. We find new, original combinations. We then release new outputs to our environment that make it healthier and stronger, able to support ever more diversity.

In contrast, those being phased out are closed off. They only receive, interact with, and combine the familiar components that already exist inside their closed, contrived worlds.

Those who live in closed worlds do not interact with the changing environment outside their worlds. Consequently, they release nothing new or useful into the environment. Since there is no cleansing flow through, toxic waste builds up within their closed lives and social systems, usually in the form of envy and resentment. Resentment leads to hate. Hate leads to violence. Those who live disconnected from God and nature poison themselves out of existence. Their way of life dies out – sometimes with a bang, but most often with a whimper.

We have no hand in the phasing out of those who refuse contact with God and creation, except to be a living alternative that proves God has a better way of living.

Day 18

Our immune system responds immediately to the presence of a pathogen, right when and where the invader appears. Our immune system does not wait to respond until it is convenient. Our wound-healing system also responds immediately to a cut or burn, right when and where it is needed. It does not wait. We are no different.

To stay open and fluid, we adjust quickly, without complaint, to changes in our surrounding situation. We do not waste time or energy trying to force our environment to adjust to us, so we can stay just as we are. There is a direct relationship between how fast we respond effectively to change in our surroundings and how long we will exist on earth.

The faster and better the response, the longer a species remains. The slower and worse the response the sooner a species ceases to exist.

Day 19

We put in the time and effort to see what others are going through and sense whether we ourselves would want to go through that, then adjust our behaviors. We don't do to another what we would never want anyone to do to us or our loved ones. When we see a situation in which we ourselves would welcome an act of helpful kindness we spontaneously offer the help we would welcome, without causing any loss of dignity.

Our empathy is what makes what we do sustainable. Acting with empathy is what God expects first and always from us as our Creator. This divine expectation is called *The Ethical Imperative*.

None of this is groundbreaking. What is different is how we use *The Ethical Imperative* when we begin to build anything new.

Day 20

When we set out to build any endeavor, we set *The Ethical Imperative* in place first, before and above all other priorities. We will let no other priority displace it. This means that every word and action is governed by empathy. We consider the reality we are creating for others and ask ourselves if we ourselves would want to live inside that reality.

Wise societies don't go cheap or fast when building roads, bridges and the culverts that divert water way from roads and inhabited areas. In the same way, we don't go cheap or fast on this critical piece of social infrastructure. We spare no effort to make sure our commitment to mutual well-being is real and robust. Words with no actions won't do.

We don't use fancy words spoken in public as a substitute for consistent behaviors no one will notice but God. Engineers don't need poetry and typically aren't very poetic. They don't need to be. What they build works. Their work speaks for them.

Day 21

No one among us is exempt from *The Ethical Imperative*. We hold our leaders accountable to protect, build and strengthen this feature of our society above all else. Any breach of *The Ethical Imperative* is grounds for immediate removal from any leadership role, no matter how difficult it is to do this. Engineers set priorities when it comes to the budget. They direct money where their math tells them to make the investment in the right materials to do the job.

We do the same kind of thing by limiting who we trust to lead to those who are the best at consistently solving problems - ethically. We have done the social math and know the horrors that follow when leaders don't follow God but chase the crowd's approval in service of their own vanity.

Our leaders have demonstrated over decades the habit of choosing God's priorities over anything else, no matter what that cost them in terms of material reward and popularity.

Day 22

To illustrate how we build a new society, imagine a large glass jar and beside it five large rocks, ten medium-sized rocks, lots of gravel and a huge pile of sand. Imagine putting the smaller rocks, gravel, and sand in first, then trying to put in the large rocks. It would not work. They would simply have to be left out.

The largest rock that we put in first – is our standing ethical commitment to the well-being of the other lives with whom we share this time and space. Only after we place this foundational value at the center do we start to put in whatever else we can and find to enhance our lives. There are some things we just must leave out because at present they cannot be included without harming others.

Building in *The Ethical Imperative* first is what allows all members of our new society to thrive individually and to function together collectively. This is the one essential difference what makes our civilization truly new and sustainable. Remove The Ethical Imperative and our society will fail just like all the others.

With a few exceptions, the civilizations that went before built everything else in first that they were sure would make them happy, then left empathy and ethics to be added at the end as a nice option, but not as a necessity. They gave elaborate lip service to ethics but never let ethics limit their greed or anger. The resulting cultures prevented each member of their society from growing into full ethical maturity and prevented individuals and groups from ever cooperating as well as they could have. When there was cooperation it was to conquer and destroy nature and other groups, not to thrive as part of nature and alongside other groups.

Day 23

Animal species can degenerate. Over successive generations a species can lose an adaptive capacity it once had. A degenerate animal will typically be smaller, weaker, and more vulnerable to harm than its ancestor. As a result, degenerate species go extinct. The penalty for degeneration is not being excluded from the most enjoyable existence. The penalty for degeneration is to be excluded from any existence whatsoever.

Since we are animals, we are no different. If we aren't using a capacity, we are losing it. If we are making ethics an option instead of an imperative, we are at this very moment losing the ability to choose and act ethically when it matters most - when it is costly.

There is a way to tell. Degenerate humans become hypersensitive to any suggestion they might be ethically dysfunctional or that there is a better way and respond very badly.

Regenerating humans can receive and respond to signals that offer ethical correction and advancement and respond very well.

Day 24

Degeneration is not the loss of a capacity an individual animal once had. Rather, degeneration has started when an individual animal never grows the capacity its ancestors used to have. The development of that capacity simply stops and does not complete itself, leaving it stunted in that area. When a stunted individual reproduces, the offspring inherit the dysfunction and live as if it is normal.

The worst case of degeneration is when a creature fails to grow something it must have to survive in its environment. An example would be an insect that grows a leg where its antennae should have been.

There are individuals who have chosen to grow cunning cruelty where cooperative empathy should have emerged. They can pretend to feel empathy, using it as a technique to disarm, mislead and harm others, but they actually have no ability to feel empathy or compassion.

In general, the shallower a person is, the better that person can pretend to be something they are not, to feel things they don't feel. Acting is a shallow art. It only requires the ability to study and mimic appearances, to appear to be something, not to be something in reality.

Acting and performing is all about how things look on the surface, not about a lifetime commitment to being a living embodiment of a set of values.

Day 25

When an actor comes to preside over a society, it is the beginning of the end.

When someone comes to control a society who is cunning and cruel, who has no capacity for empathy at all, the end has arrived.

The ascension of someone to the highest office in the land who rules through terror is our signal to go into hiding. Our task is to preserve our knowledge of how God does things, to be the living alternative to the rule of criminal madness.

And to await further instructions.

Day 26

All creatures need a safe place to regenerate, to refuel, to rest. Humans need a place to work out new solutions to what they are facing outside of their safe space. What if there is no safe space? What happens to humans when home base is as threatening and challenging as what lies outside home base? What if humans see ethics as a nice option, but as the first thing to abandon when their interests are at stake?

Under these conditions humans will not fully regenerate. They stop growing. They can't afford to grow. They need the energy continued growth would require just to protect themselves from the harm others can and will inflict on them. When humans stop growing into all God created each to be because they fear the behavior of around them – the human animal is no longer regenerating, it is degenerating.

Day 27

It is not possible to build a sustainable civilization out of degenerating individuals, any more than it would be possible to build a 20-story apartment building out of sugar cubes. The first heavy rain will bring it crashing down.

A sustainable civilization can only be built out of individuals who fully participate in the process of moral regeneration.

We stop degeneration before it starts. Since ethics is our first and constant concern, our home base works as a place of constant regeneration. People who live around us find rest, safety, and moral nourishment. They find they can refuel and retool as needed. They can afford to try new things, to grow, to learn, to change.

A culture of ethics-first and mandatory - instead of ethics-last and optional is the difference that makes all the difference, because it creates a safe place to regenerate. Ethics alone can create and preserve a safe home base. Ethics consists mostly of behaviors, not words. It is about choices, when choosing the right thing to do is the hardest. It is not about intentions.

In practical, daily terms, ethics means making and keeping agreements, following through on promises, following up on conversations and recent adjustments to see if more effort and attention is required.

Day 28

Only a culture that sees ethics as its first and mandatory feature can create safety and provide constant moral nourishment. When people are safe and nourished, their uniqueness, their talents and strengths emerge. They grow stronger, happier, and more confident.

With a safe and nourishing home base, humans, guided and directed by God, can use their amazing capacities to work together to surmount whatever challenges they face. They can unlearn, re-learn, re-fuel, and re-tool, until they have in hand the adaptive solutions their changing situation requires.

Day 29

Ethical leadership alone creates and protects a habitat of resourced safety.

Commerce has never done this. Neither science nor technology can do this. Education promises to do this, but never seems to deliver, as scholars are too absorbed in their own vicious squabbles to do much else. Entertainment dulls boredom, distracts, flatters, and soothes, but does little else besides creating self-absorbed celebrities. Religious rituals, services, and ceremonies elevate moods but not behaviors.

Legislation and court decisions come into play only after damage has been done, unable to fully restore what was lost. Written laws only set off a highly motivated search for loopholes and exceptions. Once enough people find a way around a law it becomes useless in practice. Legal systems stop little criminals, but big ones rip right through them like wet tissue paper.

Fame makes people rich and powerful, but not honorable. What famous people are best at is making themselves famous – not making others safe. Magic offers a short cut that doesn't exist – an intoxicating ride to nowhere. Great fortunes have almost always been built on great crimes against the innocent and nature.

All these enticing things are just gravel and sand in the jar. They provide no solid foundation of values for a society.

Day 30

All previous failed civilizations put their hope in alluring, but ultimately useless distractions and ignored God's ethical imperative in practice, if not in words.

We are different. We instinctively put our hope firmly in God, who is all knowing, all powerful, and present everywhere in everything always. For us it makes no sense to rest our ultimate trust in anything or anyone else.

We don't waste time repeating high sounding beautiful words. Instead, we put our attention and effort into consistently behaving in ways that are helpful and cooperative.

Memorable, pretty words don't please God. Consistent, practical, ethical behaviors please God. If we all clean out our own harmful behavior from the social space we live in, the whole earth will be cleansed and renewed.

Individually, none of us has the ability to clean out the harmful behaviors of others, although we must put a stop to it when it threatens to harm us and those we love. Even when we stop the harm others attempt to do to us, we have not stopped their desire to behave that way. It is still there and will show up again, with even greater force. The best thing we can do is put sufficient distance between ourselves and them.

Day 31

We focus on our own harmful attitudes, words, choices, habits, and behaviors. We don't wait for everyone else to do it before we start. The reset starts now, here, in my own daily actions. We don't advertise to anyone by any means that we are doing this. We aren't seeking recognition and approval from others for doing the work of regeneration. We just do it.

Even repairing the damage done by the harmful behavior of others comes later, only after we have stopped harming others ourselves, even if it was only by neglecting to help them when they needed our help in word or deed.

We have learned by experience that God honors those who take the divine ethical imperative seriously and attend to it first, foremost, constantly, no matter what the cost. Those who are loyal to God find a way to solve every practical problem they face without harming others – in the face of and all the way through every set of circumstances they face.

There is no set of circumstances that justify suspending *The Ethical Imperative*. It is in precisely the most difficult circumstances that we must demonstrate most clearly our loyalty to God's rule.

Day 32

It is in the most difficult circumstances that we must choose what we value most and embody that highest value in our actions, not our words. If we don't, our "highest value" becomes a joke, and everyone knows it. When things got tough we proved ourselves to be no different than those that went before us, those who created unsustainable civilizations at war with life.

Sustainability is all about what values we ultimately stand for precisely when standing for those values is the most difficult and costly.

God acts decisively in history to protect and sustain only what was built from the very beginning to honor and embody the divine mandate for justice in all our activities, then constantly renewed and rebuilt to keep doing so.

Among us the innocent will not be harmed and living systems will not be destroyed. Among us those who harm the innocent and destroy living systems will be held accountable.

Day 33

Those who harm others must personally and immediately repair the harm they have done at their own expense, if they intend to remain among us, enjoying the peace we have worked so hard to create.

Those who harm living systems must immediately stop and immediately begin to fully repair the damage that they have done - at their own expense and effort. We will inspect the repair work. No short cuts or cheap substitutes will be accepted.

Since our social immune system is patterned after our bodies' immune system, no delay or excuse will be tolerated. If they do not respond to our rebuke they will be banned and will not receive any aid or comfort from us. We will not be complicit in crimes against life of any kind, for any reason, for any amount of time, anywhere we have control or influence over what happens.

Until we do have control or influence, we do everything we can to minimize how much we use products and services that exist by harming life. We know we cannot both condemn a product or service while using it, as we ourselves are helping to create the very demand the product or service is meeting at a profit.

Day 34

Among us, those who still harm the innocent will have no standing and no voice when it is time to solve problems and make decisions. They will have to earn their way back to a place at the table by abandoning their harmful behaviors and adopting ethical ones instead. Words alone will not do. New behaviors alone will count.

Our discipline is not to punish, but to correct behavior until it is reliably ethical. The reason is simple - God not only holds individuals accountable for their ethical lapses; God holds groups even more accountable because they can do so much more harm than individuals.

God does not just reward individuals for their ethical behavior, God also rewards groups for their collective ethical behavior – even more so, because groups can do so much more good than individuals. The reward is peace – both within the individual soul and between individuals and groups. We sleep well.

Only that which God initiates, guides, corrects and protects becomes something sustainable. That which God did not initiate, and cannot guide or correct, God will not protect, making it unsustainable. The reason is simple: all ungodly systems make ethics a nice option, so they always end up ripping themselves apart. God does nothing to save them because it is too late. They should have sought God's involvement long ago.

Day 35

Regenerating our fullest ethical capacity is essential for human endeavors to be sustained by God's constant directing, correcting presence. God will not be present with those who are currently harming others. We must stop harming first before we seek and find God.

Regenerating starts alone by making quiet, direct contact with God, informed by the vast wisdom embodied in nature. But regeneration stops and sours if it remains a solitary religious experience. Regeneration is real when it activates and strengthens the natural empathy we feel when seeing others suffering pain or loss.

Regeneration can only complete itself in a social context, in the way we treat others in our lives, especially when our interests differ from theirs, and when they are very different from us. If we treat being different as a crime we are degenerating.

If we treat being different as a natural and necessary part of creation, we are regenerating.

Day 36

Only in a social context do we see the amazing, divine function of our regenerated, natural capacities as humans. It is a function we cannot experience alone.

Generosity, kindness, and inclusion, directed at those who are different from us, sets loose a flourishing of unforeseen diversity in thought, ways of life, points of view, methods, and solutions. From this swelling reservoir of viable options new combinations can be tried and the most fruitful ones passed on.

Like what starts to emerge around a beaver bond, God's delight in what we are doing is marked by peace and sustainable sufficiency. There is little if any luxury for the few, but there is no want for the many. There is very little, if any, waste. Everything in nature is recycled and reused repeatedly.

No one is deprived. No one is coddled. No one coasts. Everyone pulls their own weight. Everyone pitches in to help do the bigger, harder things that no individual can do alone.

We use wisdom and carefulness first to solve our problems, not money. This gives everyone a part in problem-solving, equal to their capacity to understand the situation. With true understanding in hand, everyone can act with skill and persistence.

Day 37

When two parts of a living system that sustain each other are separated from each other, both parts get sick. Once they get sick, the sickness acts to separate them further from each other, which makes them sicker, which drives them further apart - forming a vicious cycle.

We stay directly connected to God, to nature, and to each other. Healing, creative information passes through this living connection. There is no other effective conduit through which this information can pass, so we do not allow disconnection. We do not seek or accept anything or anyone that claims to create for us our connection to God, or to nature, or to each other.

There is no such thing as a mediator between us and God. Just as we must breathe and eat and drink for ourselves, we must make direct contact with God on our own, inspired and informed by nature's vast intelligence.

Day 38

Sustaining this constant state of directing, correcting contact with God, nature, and each other, is what makes everything else we do sustainable. Nothing else can do that. Anything else is something less than and different from how God does sustainability. Not developing this connection in the first place, or replacing it with some human institution, was the fatal founding mistake of all previous, doomed civilizations.

By cultivating and protecting this vital, intimate connection, we learn how God does and does not work among us. God does not have a plan. God has a way. God's way guides all problem-solving and decision-making through all circumstances and situations, leading always to an ever-expanding field of justice, inclusion, diversity, and creativity. God's way is a lot of things, but one thing it is not is boring, predictable, or tedious.

Our living connection to God, to nature, and to each other keeps us synchronized, like a band with all musicians playing different parts to the same beat, even as they go off on a playful, surprising, new spontaneous improvisation. Being synchronized with God is all about timing, nuance, subtle signals and following our Leader. We follow more by feel than by sight. We learn how to wait and watch, when to initiate activity and when to stop, when to speed up and when to slow down, when to get loud and when to fall silent.

Day 39

To live sustainably we manage fear differently.

Think about the fear we naturally feel at the edge of a cliff. We fear falling from a great height. No one taught us that fear; it came pre-loaded into our brains at birth. The fear of falling is a fear given to us by God. It protects us from unnecessary, avoidable harm ahead of time. God-given fear is healthy, sane, and productive. It keeps us moving and moving in the right direction. It stops us before we do harm to ourselves or others. It keeps us alive.

With a fear given by God, there is always a way to deal with the object of our fear effectively and early enough to prevent harm, if we listen to hear the wisdom in the fear.

God-given fear tells us about our natural limits and vulnerabilities and what will happen if we go beyond our limits and expose our vulnerabilities. God-given fear is the root of wisdom – which is all the ways we stay within our natural limits and manage our vulnerabilities in a way that does not make the situation worse.

Day 40

God-given fear prompts us to add the variable of time to the equation before we make an irreversible choice about what to do now.

God-given fear teaches us to see how a given option works out in the long-term, not just how it works out in the near-term. At some point we will all arrive in the long-term situation set in motion by our choices now.

Unsustainable civilizations attempted to become invulnerable and to have no limits on their greed or anger. What they ended up with was massive, expensive, complicated systems which were unstable – creating dread, which is very different than God-given fear.

Dread is when we fear something real, but we are powerless to do anything about it, because there is no effective timely action available.

Anything humans attempt when their massive unstable systems start to fail is always too little too late. In attempting to live without natural, manageable fear in small, passing doses, humans end up living with unnatural, unmanageable, big, inescapable, permanent doses of fear.

Day 41

Seeing huge surpluses of material resources, popular support, and advanced knowledge at first makes humans feel smug and invulnerable. They feel they have escaped what all other creatures must contend with. They feel they no longer need God, as they have something far better than God – they have what they need and the promise of more of what they need for forever. Besides, they can control this horde of resources in a way that they could not hope to control God.

It is a hallucination to believe that having *more* of what we desire and holding on to it forever is the recipe for happiness. It is not. It is the recipe for paranoia because we must fear others trying to take what we are trying to hold onto. Paranoia is different from God-given fear.

Having *enough*, perfectly fitted to the moment, shared between others who are cooperative and there to help – this is the recipe for both happiness and sustainability.

Ours is a contingent way of living, but one of constant wonder, gratitude, contentment, and lightness that allows us to be gracious and generous.

Day 42

We don't set use systems that consume more resources than our immediate natural environment can re-replenish through its normal seasons and cycles.

Living daily in the presence of God and within small, local cooperative groups, we need less to be happy in the first place, so we don't need to demand more of our environment than it can re-replenish and stay healthy.

We do not set up systems of imagination and greed that blind us to the limits of our environment. We have a natural, God-given fear that stops us from overusing or damaging our environment. That includes our social environment. We don't assume we can hurt or neglect other lives and still count on them for help when we need it.

Day 43

Most of the time, we meet our own needs and feel dignity in our ability to do that. But we also do nothing to harm the trust and goodwill of those whose help we ourselves will need at a moment when we can't meet a need completely on our own.

Our sustainable way of life is an elegant combination of mostly individual creative independence, some cooperative interdependence, and occasional, brief periods of unavoidable dependence on others – when we are children, when we are sick or injured and when we are old. This pattern is observable in all successful, long-lived social species. It is the embodiment of the wisdom of God and is energized by the natural, God-given fear of trying to survive alone through all the challenges life brings over time without any reliable help from others.

Unsustainable ways of life reverse this natural ratio, creating an ugly combination of mostly life-long, servile dependence on huge, impersonal systems, some grudging interdependence with others, and brief spurts of playful independence, mostly in adolescence.

Day 44

The reason we don't try to banish necessary, natural, healthy fear from our lives is that fear alone has the power to summon forces in our brains that otherwise lie dormant.

If you have ever walked a dog in a place where there are deer you will notice that the deer may stay near where you are walking and just watch you and your dog. They can tell whether your dog is off leash and is a real threat or is on a leash and is not a real threat. They must get through hard winters when there is little food available. They can't afford to waste energy running from something that cannot and will not chase them or harm them.

In a similar way, our brains usually will not waste energy finding practical solutions for abstract, imagined threats. This is the reason people hate being forced to do role plays in training classes. The exercises are contrived and rarely create new skills and habits that will kick in automatically when needed.

Day 45

By staying in touch with our real limits and natural vulnerabilities, we keep open the circuits of real learning and adjusting. If we create huge systems to protect us from ever needing to unlearn, re-learn and adjust to dynamic, changing situations we lose those abilities altogether. If we let our natural fear circuits decay by always avoiding fear, we will be paralyzed at the very moment we must respond with courage, precision, and skill.

By contrast, when our natural, God-given fear circuits are functioning normally we quickly pull ourselves together when the situation demands it, and we rapidly modify our methods.

We simplify what is too complicated, we streamline what is too cumbersome.

We complete what has been left unfinished and thus useless.

We tighten what is too loose to respond effectively to the real threats in our situation. We speed up what is too slow to respond fast enough to be effective.

We warm up the parts of ourselves that are too cold and hard to feel anything. We cool down the parts that are too hot to respond calmly and precisely.

Day 46

Our bodies can only use water in its liquid form. Our bodies can't make productive use of ice or steam. Our social behaviors are very similar. We are useless socially if we are too cold and indifferent or too hot.

Enough God-given fear does for our ever-flowing minds what a little salt does for water.

With just enough salt in the mix, water can get to a much colder temperature before it freezes. We can put up with a lot more before we just don't care anymore, and even then we can't stay indifferent for long. With salt in the mix water can get to a much higher temperature before it boils into steam. We can put up with a lot more before we lose our temper, and even then we quickly return to a calm state.

Enough God-given fear expands the range and duration of our usefulness – into far more situations than we could enter otherwise, and farther out in time than our influence could extend otherwise. The wisdom that comes from God-given fear makes us careful, attentive, and precise, in ways we could not be if we felt smug and comfortable.

Day 47

To live sustainably we live in a fluid state of mind, with flexible and adaptive behaviors, not a rigid state of mind, with fixed and unresponsive behaviors.

In striking contrast to the liquid state of water and it can do, think about the static state of a statue and what it can and can't do. It has eyes but cannot see you. It has ears but cannot hear you. It has a nose but cannot smell anything in the room. It has hands that do not feel your touch. Its surface is cold and hard, not warm, and supple.

A statue is an imagined, frozen representation of life. It is not life. Stone was once the favorite medium people used to represent life or lofty ideas, including God. More recently, lifeless representations of life have used the medium of digital bits, not stone, but the same thing is going on – false representations designed to enrich the few at the expense of the many.

Day 48

It is false to use statues or any other human-created representations to model how life works or how to participate in creation. Man-made artful representations can appear lifelike, but they have none of the defining features of life because they cannot and do not interact with their actual, immediate, complete environment.

Those who admire human creations and see them as the embodiment of ultimate truth come to resemble the representations they admire. Admiring a human creation more than creation itself and The Creator's wisdom is a sure sign of advanced degeneration. Those in an advanced state of degeneration become fixated, repetitious, cold, proud, and blind to the suffering of those around them. Like a statue or a digital product, the degenerate exist to attract attention, not to give attention.

We don't try to be like or participate in any human representations of life, whether material or virtual. Instead, we work daily to stay warm, responsive, and flexible, fully alive to our actual, unique, particular situation. We don't miss the dynamic details to be found our natural and social surroundings. God is met in the flowing, changing details, not in any fixed, generalized abstraction.

Day 49

When we live in a fluid, warm, receptive, and responsive state we choose our behaviors to meet the needs of the situation, keeping the ethical imperative at the top of priorities.

When we respond ethically and creatively in a unique, unforeseen way, our behavior changes the situation we are responding to into a new situation, which itself requires a new response that is first ethical, then practical and productive.

To stay in a fluid state, we live in a creative feedback loop. Our fresh, original actions change the situation which requires fresh, original changes in our actions, which changes the situation into a new one. And so on, and so on. Everything changes except change itself - and our ethical response to change. There are a few principles of life that never change. There is an endless succession of new, combined methods that constantly change.

The way we live is like a river. The destination of rivers remains the same over millennia. Where the banks are located changes regularly, but what never changes is the fact that there are two banks limiting and directing the flow of water, one on each side. The water that flows through the river, and the makeup of the things the water carries along constantly change through replacement.

Day 50

God's daily presence in our minds keeps us in a fluid state, ready to receive and respond to divine inspection and constant course corrections. Back when cholera ravaged crowded cities doctors prescribed the "water cure." Patients were sent out to the country and told to drink only pure spring water for weeks. The spring water had no pathogens or parasites in it, so the body got a break from constantly being re-infected every day. Without the constant assault the immune system could take it from there and do its amazing work.

An infected "healer" is not a healer at all, but rather a super-spreader, someone who passes on the sickness to those who are already weakened, but in far greater numbers than someone who has no reputation as a healer. Institutions set up to mediate between humans and God always end up being super-spreaders of the worst moral diseases, justifying harmful behavior in the name of God.

Like the spring water, for us to function on earth the way God intended, we must carry none of the old pathogens or parasites in our values, attitudes, words, behaviors, and unplanned reactions to whatever we encounter. Candles and costumes are ethically useless. There is no ritual or ceremony that can make us pure and benign.

We must know how to work with God to dislodge and flush out our own sickness. We must know first-hand how God does change and regeneration. It takes years, not hours. It happens in our ordinary, daily lives in relationship with others around us, not in special "holy" places on "holy" days. All the failed civilizations before us used those gimmicks in place of real repentance and return to God's rule. We will not repeat that mistake.

Day 51

We live in a feedback loop that is different from the feedback loops that exist in unsustainable societies. Our feedback loops are open, not closed, like the river that constantly receives new, fresh water. We are not like a stagnant pond or salt sea that can only circulate the old, polluted water that is already there. Stagnant ponds breed disease carrying pests. Salt seas can sustain very few species, if any.

To sustain constant renewal, we seek and gain daily input from God in the form of the ethical way to solve practical problems. Then we seek and gain input from the models we see in the ways nature solves the complex problems that come with living in a changing environment.

In time, we see a pattern. We can sense how God's ethical input and what we see in nature complement each other. Then we seek input from the small, local social unit that we support and that supports us about how we might apply the pattern we see to our situation.

When these inputs all converge to support a proposed solution, we move forward. When we are confused and these inputs don't agree, we stop and wait for the situation to clarify itself.

Day 52

Clarity often emerges from the background of confusion It comes in an event that is unplanned, unforeseen, and unglamorous, but which creates an opening.

Through the opening we see that we can and should move into our situation with a wise, kind, and ethical deed. Real deeds have no need to announce themselves ahead of time or praise themselves afterwards.

Only in real deeds responding to real needs does the rule of God on earth become real and convincing, the way a series of experiments in science can confirm the accuracy of one theory over another.

Day 53

We solve the problems we face together, *together* – face to face, through consensus, not through voting to find the majority opinion.

Decisions that are supported only by the authority of math (reaching 51%) do not create peace. The majority dominates the minority.

Domination is not cooperation. Domination can only achieve resentful compliance at best, not commitment. Without commitment there is no initiative and innovation. Instead, people do just enough to avoid getting in trouble with the majority, but no more.

To achieve majority status a group uses salesmanship, bribes, and threats, all of which can be delivered in mass at a distance.

In contrast, to achieve true, lasting consensus, people must know they were truly seen and heard. To do this we must know each other's track record personally, listen to each other deeply with our ears and eyes, and reason together fairly, using facts and logic.

We must already have in place a shared history of lessons learned together, directly, and personally - the hard way.

To reach true consensus is to coalescence around something higher, around interests that include but transcend our individual interests. Setting our sights higher becomes more natural the more we each have experienced God's intervention in our shared situation in ways that completely changed what was possible.

We must have first learned that that divine intervention is normal and leads to the best solutions the facts of the situation will allow. This sets the standard for the next solution we seek. It becomes normal to factor in divine involvement when we solve complex problems together.

Day 54

There is a hard limit to how large and concentrated a population can be and still govern itself by true consensus. This is why we leave massive aggregations of people and instead, form small, local groups for the purpose of solving problems that impact us all. We can then maintain and improve the solutions we created together, guided by God and inspired by nature.

When one of our solutions breaks down we know how to fix it ourselves, because we made it ourselves. When it needs improving or replacing, we can do that ourselves too.

The Ethical Imperative demands that we replace old solutions that don't work anymore while still honoring those who built them. We know those who worked out or maintained past solutions personally. We don't want to take from them the gratitude they have earned. One day our new solutions will be old too and will need to be replaced. We treat those who served us well in the past the way we want to be treated in the future.

Above all, we reason with each other, staying within in a mandatory, ethics-first frame of mind. We accept together the limits God has placed on the way we treat each other as we work through any challenge we face.

There is no set of circumstances that warrants suspending God's ethical mandate.

Day 55

God's justice exists and can be learned. Once learned, God' justice can guide and limit each person's behavior from the inside out, willingly, spontaneously, and constantly. As each of us governs ourselves within the limits of God's justice, we naturally choose not to harm each other, regardless of what that choice costs us. We naturally choose to help each other, even when it is inconvenient. The result is an ever-increasing, peaceful, interesting, surprising, and productive excellence. We create a steady stream of new and different solutions that are better than those we used in the past. Replacement and upgrade are normal in nature, so it is normal among us.

This social excellence is a living thing of beauty. Peaceful, constantly evolving beauty is the signature of God. Peaceful beauty is visible proof of the presence of the invisible God. Our lives, individually and collectively, make the invisible visible.

Day 56

The way we manage fear leads to courage. We learn what to fear most of all – losing our constant connection to God and the ethical guidance it provides. We learn that compared to that loss, all other losses are manageable and usually avoidable.

We have learned that by staying committed to God's purposes and abiding by God's ethical imperative, we stay linked to God through everything we encounter. God has not abandoned us when we remained loyal to God's rule. God will not abandon us now or in the future as long as we remain connected, receptive, and responsive to God's inspection, correction, and direction. This is the source of our courage. No human gave it to us. No human can take it from us.

Day 57

The way we manage anger is also central to living sustainably.

Unmanaged anger is the leading cause of death for civilizations, whether large or small, old, or new. Historically, words or deeds motivated by anger, untampered by wisdom, have destroyed decades or centuries of constructive work, causing a society to implode and vanish into oblivion.

Anger is about goals and attachment. When a goal is blocked we get angry. Anger is a gift from God. It is a vital source of energy. But anger is not God. Anger cannot direct itself and will not limit itself. Undirected, anger is uselessly destructive. Unchanneled anger wastes courage while producing nothing useful for the future.

While anger is *not* God, anger can be *from* God and used for God's purposes. Therefore, we don't deny or suppress our anger, we bring it to God, quietly, in solitude. It is natural and healthy to be angry at what God never endorsed and does not support. But only God knows how to displace injustice with justice. God will not ask us to give up our anger, or to forgive before there has been any remorse before harmful behavior has been renounced and abandoned by those around us.

Instead, God guides us to become living proof that unjust living is unnecessary. Our lives become stubborn facts. The way we behave offers evidence that there is another way of living together on earth which shows that any alternative is self-defeating by comparison.

Day 58

Unjust, harmful, uncooperative, selfish, spiteful, arrogant ways of living combine to form a massive dam across the river of life.

Our undeniable living alternative is like the first crack in the dam.

It starts as a trickle, but each drop of water that seeps through carries away a little bit of the dam, which opens the crack wider, which lets in more water, which erodes more of the dam - until the trickle becomes an unstoppable torrent.

The life God first created on earth has never died out. It divided into new paths that divided repeatedly, eventually producing all of us. Like the river, life cannot be stopped, and its ultimate trajectory will not be altered.

Life has direction, a goal. It always leads to more of itself by creating more and different versions of itself. Life itself always finds a way through or around any obstacles and destroys anything that seeks to prevent it from becoming whatever it will become next.

Day 59

Yes – the stopping, the damming up of justice makes us mad, as it should. As it must. We don't side with the dam. We side with the river because we know which is going to succeed and which is going to fail.

We channel our anger daily, under precise, divine direction, into original, creative choices. Our ethical choices open the future so life can continue expanding and diversifying. We act in concert with The Creator's purposes, and in return, The Creator brings the full force of natural forces to bear to support and extend our creative actions.

The best revenge is to survive to live at a higher level of complexity than those who harmed us.

Only God can bring about the best revenge – the complete replacement of what God never wanted with all that God intends for earth. As we embrace the ways God does things and see the results we start to replace more of what we used to do with natural ways of solving problems that don't create more problems.

It is not long before we have a system of functioning solutions that is incompatible with the system we were born into. We must choose between them. It is not that hard to choose. As what God has directed us to build begins to thrive, what the culture around us has built it starting to implode.

Day 60

Water follows the course of least resistance. It finds the weakest, most vulnerable spot in the dam. We do the same thing. We pay close attention to what is happening in the lives of those around us and meet needs the doomed, godless civilization cannot and will not meet.

We sense the pain that is common to the human experience and apply our kindness there, when there is no praise or profit in doing so. We see those who are invisible otherwise. We hear those who no one listens to otherwise. We help those who can do nothing for us in return.

Loneliness creates fissures across the entire structure of the dam. The dam makes a few people famous, rich, and powerful, but at the cost of making everyone else lonely and afraid.

The lonely heart is a sick heart. Loneliness is the accurate perception that it is highly unlikely one will ever be able to create a mutually supportive, reciprocally helpful relationship, given how people behave whenever their selfishness is frustrated in any way,

We touch loneliness at its core simply by existing as the kind of person with whom it is not only possible, but likely, to build a safe home base, a place of repair and renewal.

Day 61

Our very existence is a threat to any godless, doomed civilization, so we do nothing to draw attention to ourselves or make any public claim to righteousness or wisdom. Rather, we simply behave differently in every interaction with any other creature God put on earth, right where we are, right now, and do so constantly.

The water of justice never stops flowing through our lives, so it never stops flowing through us creating an ever-larger crack in the dam. The river of life never stops getting stronger and the dam of death never stops getting weaker.

The river is sustainable by its very nature. The dam is unsustainable by its very nature. Time is on the side of life. Time is the mortal enemy of the selfish and systems built on selfishness. Life itself is what God sustains, not any particular form of life. To participate in what God sustains, for as long as our species exists, is what is means to live sustainably.

We won't go on forever, but life will – in ever new and different forms. We will live on encoded in the genes of whatever comes next, which we can't foresee, control or exploit. Life passes through us, but it is not about us.

What God will sustain is the direction, the trajectory of life toward ever greater diversity of form and function.

Day 62

God's creation has a goal, but it is not to make us individually happy by being soaked in pleasure, at ease without any worries. God does nothing to sustain a human-centered civilization or a self-centered life. God is not the source of individualistic, self-centered religions, therapies, or philosophies. Nor does God protect and sustain a political system organized around what one group of humans wants, at the expense of all the others.

God set up reality to organize itself, but not around our whims or fantasies, either individually or collectively. In God's design, life organizes itself around what is most sustainable as the environment around it changes.

For social species, what is most sustainably cooperative is the most sustainable. Forms of cooperation that constantly fall apart were never from God in the first place. Forms of cooperation that constantly renew, strengthen, and improve themselves are from God, just as we see in nature.

Day 63

When we organize our lives around God's calling, around what God wants, we are constantly met, taught, prompted, and assisted at critical moments. We are constantly surprised and amazed, but at the same time we know this is normal for those who are loyal to God and give up whatever they must to stay loyal.

We are only as strong as we are at our weakest point and most wobbly moment. If we fail there and then, our efforts will come to nothing.

As we struggle through our weakest, most vulnerable times, we emerge with an even stronger connection to God's ethical guidance and even more earned confidence. We know by experience that we have an ability to cooperate with God.

We can sense that the way we have learned to behave will make it into the future somehow, in some form, allowing those who come after us to survive and thrive under circumstances we can only vaguely imagine. It is the way of life. Successful new responses to environmental stresses are passed on, stored in the life history of those who saved themselves by using the new responses. Unsuccessful, outlived responses to environmental stresses die with those who wasted their lives using those unfit responses in the face of ample evidence that their behaviors did not solve the problems they face.

Day 64

The main reason non-regenerating humans persist in using ultimately unsuccessful responses to environmental stresses is the power of desire. Our way of living is sustainable because we manage desire differently.

There are desires that come from God, and desires that come from living apart from God. There is no ultimately successful way to manage desires that come from living apart from God. Once we learn to stay connected to God, those unhealthy desires fade and drop away or are transformed into healthy desires that can be managed successfully.

The key thing to understand is that desire of any kind is a source of stored energy, like a coiled spring. It is not by itself a reliable source of direction or correction.

Our strong, live-affirming, life-long desires are a gift from God, just like healthy fear and anger. Healthy, strong desire is part of having a calling, but it is different from having a calling. We are not called to gratify our desires. We are called to implement God's desires. We do not turn our desires into a god we sacrifice everything to obey.

Since our desires are essential for life, we don't try to extinguish them. Instead, we bring them to God and acknowledge that we don't know best how to manage them.

Day 65

We acknowledge that no desire, no matter how strong, can direct our choices and behaviors because desire is not God, desire is from God for God's purposes. We have learned that our desires function to energize and sustain our choices and behaviors. We ask God to harness, refine, and direct our desires. Then we stand ready to respond daily to all God does to make that happen in our souls. It does not happen fast, but it sure happens.

When God harnesses and directs our desires we find over time, to our surprise, a lasting contentment and satisfaction we never imagined could be possible.

Feeling deeply satisfied inside frees us to move on from using old responses to the challenges we face in our environment. Now we can put our attention and energy, undistracted, into finding new and better responses.

Day 66

Insatiable desire that treats itself as if it were God is a mark of degeneration. "I want" is the beginning of every form of magic and idolatry. Idolatry is worshiping what humans made as if it is divine. Magic is using the divine as a gimmick to get what I want. You will never find idolatry without magic nearby or magic without idolatry nearby. Vices cluster in predictable ways. When you see one you know the others are close by.

Those who are not regenerating find when they get what they wanted and worked for, it does not truly satisfy or satisfy for long. Insatiable desire is a cancer that eats us alive from the inside out. Insatiable desire also ruins all our relationships because we come to see others as either just a tool to satisfy our desires, or an obstacle to getting what we want.

The religion, philosophy, psychology, politics, and economics of those who do not seek God and are not regenerating can be summed up in the idol called MORE.

Insatiability is the driving force behind all that is doomed and unsustainable in human civilization. At some point the natural and social environment cannot replenish the resources consumed to constantly satisfy the god of MORE. More of everything never satisfies and never will.

Yet we are insatiable for a reason.

Day 67

Only an unlimited, ever-expanding, present, tangible reality can satisfy the unlimited, ever-expanding longings of the human soul. No theory can do that.

The only reality that can satisfy is the living, daily presence of God that we meet, not in contrived, mood-elevating ritual, but in the daily experience of ethical and practical problem-solving. We know the Creator intimately only by joining the process of creation, on its own terms, using the methods it has used and refined for billions of years. Working together creates satisfying intimacy between minds that nothing else can.

Knowing God's presence through active participation in creation brings us to a place of unpredictable, yet frequent moments of awe and gratitude. These moments push out selfishness, arrogance and spite and draw in kindness, humility, cooperation, and generosity, resulting in peace of mind and peaceful, productive relationships.

Day 68

Our way of living is sustainable because we use imagination differently.

Among those not regenerating, it is normal to start life wild and free and end life tame and servile. By contrast, we start life largely tamed and cowed by the power of the doomed civilization around us and end our lives in a newly wild state, free to create what has always been possible under different conditions, but never yet created.

As God changes us from the inside out, we find ourselves increasingly free *from* the false demands of the culture we were born into, and free *for* the work God put us here to do. Any other kind of freedom is a mirage. It is false freedom that leads to real mental, emotional and material enslavement.

The remarkable counter cultural journey of return, back into earth's natural history ensues naturally as we relearn how to use the capacity for curiosity, which is shared by many creatures, and combine it with the unique human capacity of imagination.

Day 69

Imagination can foreshadow and precede a missing and needed creation. With our imaginations we can sense that the situation could be different than it is. Most of the useful things we enjoy every day were once only something someone imagined, they did not yet exist in reality. Someone, or some group of people, had to bring the new useful creation into existence.

If we imagine gaining an advantage for ourselves or our group at the cost of harming others, we are degenerate. God will not be present with us. God will not be involved in our endeavors, as they are pathways to death.

We are free to choose what we do but we are not free to choose the consequences of what we do. If harming others to get everything we want is the way we choose to use our freedom there will be complications and problems for which there are no solutions.

The natural consequences of misusing our imagination will erase us, our freedom, and our societies from the community of life earth.

Day 70

In contrast, if we use our imagination to envision ways all of us could benefit together with no harm to other lives, we are regenerating. God will meet us along the way by touch, with a quiet gentle voice. By using our imaginations only to further God's love of life in all its diversity, we can be sure of God's presence and help.

God will provide useful timely information to aid the work. God will arrange unforeseen events that open what was a closed set of conditions. Our work will move on through to its fulfillment, leaving death and decay behind, as the door of opportunity closes behind us and new vistas of possibly open ahead of us.

There is no more rewarding or fulfilling way to live. We would never even consider going back to the way we used to use our imaginations, because what we experience now is beyond anything we could ever have imagined. We have entered the holy workspace of God's imagination.

Life is open-ended and always finds a new, novel way into the future. Life already has a way of doing this and is underway using it. If we remain fascinated by, and attentive to, the genius of life, remain curious and use our imaginations to anticipate where life might be headed, while staying subject to ethical correction, we get to be there when life performs its next astounding feat of survival and growth.

Day 71

We were created as free creatures with free choice. Yet we are not free to choose the consequences of our choices. We can choose to do things life's way on life's terms, or we can choose to do something else. If we do something else we put ourselves on a different path – one that goes nowhere. Our lives and our way of life will simply peter out into nothingness, like a river that has been so overused upstream that it no longer reaches the ocean but narrows to a trickle and finally ends in a dry wash in the desert. By willful mismanagement, not only is the river lost, but all the abundance and diversity of life that would have grown around it is lost as well.

All that life could still create, but hasn't yet, belongs to God. That rich field of possibility is not ours to do with as we please. If we destroy what life could have created before it gets a chance to do so, we could very well end up eliminating what we ourselves will need to survive in a future we can't predict. We will have gotten exactly what we deserve.

Justice is built into the ways of life.

Day 72

The best way to stay part of life is to stay engaged in life's way of doing things on life's terms. To stay engaged in life is to first reject what is not part of life's way of doing things.

Stuff does not make us happy, and it never has for any length of time. Ritual does not make us holy, and it never has - at all.

God created us to be happy and holy, individually, and collectively.

To be happy means to be lucky - to feel like life is going our way, because finally we are going life's way. To be lucky is to be met by life in the most delightful and surprising ways, consistently, opening new and wonderful possibilities for creation. It is a feeling of triumph - when a newly-cultivated capacity overcomes a long-standing, frustrating barrier. It is the feeling of God-given freedom.

To be holy means to be whole, to be completely functional. It is to have no capacity missing that we need to perform our function on earth, and to have nothing extra added that contributes nothing to our function on earth. Extra baggage and complications, which always accompany the pursuit of stuff and ritual, just consume time and effort without adding anything to the stock of happiness we can all draw upon.

Day 73

Happiness and holiness complete each other, forming a virtuous cycle. True happiness produces holiness, and true holiness produces a greater stock of happiness for all of life on earth.

A happy and holy people will endure as part of earth for as long as God needs them to continue the story of life, God's master work. That is all it means to live sustainably; to stick around and perform our function well for as long as we are needed for a purpose we can't fully know.

Without an ever-growing, experience-based confidence in God's wisdom and goodness, it is not possible to live this way. We must entrust our future to God and depend upon God willingly without knowing exactly how it will all work out or what rewards lie in story for us.

The experience of fulfillment, meaning, and deep satisfaction will be unique for each of us, because each of us is unique. It cannot be bottled, mass-produced, and sold. Only cheap substitutes can be.

Each of our lives is to be a unique, never-before heard, never-again repeated note in the vast symphony of life on earth.

Day 74

Humans live unsustainably because we are insatiable. Nothing is ever enough. Humans just must have more of everything, until we exceed the capacity of our natural environment to renew itself.

For humans to create a sustainable civilization, we must trust that since God made our brains, God alone knows how to satisfy the infinite longings we have inside. What we long for is our Infinite Creator's presence, and that presence is only found in fulfilling our practical function as part of a living system.

Stuff and rituals can flatter and soothe us temporarily, but they always leave behind an even bigger hole in our souls, a deeper ache for the truly eternal.

Day 75

Willing cooperation is essential for a social species to meet the challenges of a changing environment. Willing cooperation yields initiative, innovation, and nimbleness. Willing cooperation is essence of true teamwork.

A project that claims to one day secure our shared future but can be done with or without willing cooperation is not natural. It will end up creating a bigger problem than it solves. Gaining coordinated effort using incentives or threats is different from willing cooperation and it is not something to be trusted.

As soon as the incentive or threat goes away, so does the coordinated effort. As soon as someone offers a bigger incentive or makes a bigger, scarier credible threat, he or she can quickly direct effort toward a different goal. All effort on the previous goal will stop.

Appealing to greed or fear to gain cooperation is not the way true teams are formed.

Day 76

True teamwork starts with a calling from God. We sense there is a value that is higher than selfishness that must be enacted if it is to become real and effective in the life of earth. We also sense that enacting that value will require accomplishing something beyond what any one of us can do alone. To fulfill a calling, we must form a high-functioning team with those who feel the same calling pulling them out of the culture around them and up to a new, higher level of human life.

It is true teamwork that creates real friendship. It is true teamwork that reveals our true intentions and skills. True teamwork requires trust in each other's intentions and competence, and to pull together as a unit, we must each imagine and pull toward a future shared advantage, not just a personal one.

Day 77

We must each work to become more competent and confident, so our teammates can trust us to take on more responsibility. We must each become more approachable, flexible, and responsive so others want us involved in problem solving. Our reputation precedes us.

We become more competent, confident, and trustworthy by doing small things for many years in a great way. Until we can consistently bring great values to a small task, we will bring petty values to any great task we might undertake and poison it.

Supposedly "great work" that is done for petty reasons is inevitably revealed by history to be a sham. When calculated pettiness makes a mockery of high-sounding values it isn't pettiness that a society jettisons, rather it is the belief that higher values exist and actually do anything in moments of crisis.

Values lose value, values lose their good reputation, through organized and systematic hypocrisy. In nothing is this more evident than in the value attached to the word "God."

A big part of our work is to restore the reputation of God, sullied by those who claimed God's name while living contrary to God's ethical demands in pursuit of fame, power and stuff.

Day 78

To restore the name of God we start small. We learn to bring great values to small tasks. We enrich and ennoble ordinary life. We create a mystery for others that demands a satisfactory explanation. Why would anyone do small things with great care, patience, and precision when no one is watching and there will be no praise or profit in it?

The explanation for such an unexpected, seemingly irrational behavior is that God must be real to us and rules in our hearts until we do small things guided and corrected by great values. A lifetime of doing small things in a great way makes living this way habitual. A deeply instilled habit of godly excellence makes it possible and more likely we will someday bring great values to a great task, should one be entrusted to us.

When a great task is accomplished and maintained in a great way it demonstrates that God exists, can be present and real to us, and can rule in our collective endeavors by ruling first in our individual souls.

Day 79

Teamwork is the acid test of the virtues only true godliness can produce. What happens between us and our teammates is a direct reflection of what is happening right now between us and our Creator, and between us and nature.

Any word, deed or attitude that harms the team we belong to limits or stops what can be done in service of God's purposes. Any word, deed or attitude that protects and builds the team we belong to expands the possibilities of what God can do through us.

What happens between us accurately predicts what will happen around us and through us.

Day 80

Rituals often happen on a stage and what happens between the players backstage is very different from the show produced on stage. Backstage behavior is team behavior and can be an ugly contradiction of the high-sounding values espoused on stage.

Anything performed on a stage is a set up for this kind of hypocrisy and misinformation. The action on stage goes by so fast it is easy for the one who wrote the script to slip in lies and half-truths, knowing they will never be caught and corrected.

Those lies and half-truths, when believed and acted upon, always benefit those currently in power by teaching audiences to accept uncritically the way things are, as the way they must be.

Day 81

The solution to the problems caused by seeking inspiration and direction from staged performances of any kind is simple: Don't have any stages to perform on in the first place. Nowhere in nature do thousands of one species gather to watch the performances of a few of the species. Clearly life didn't require such spectacles to get this far.

All the world is not a stage, despite what we have been told. Neither the earth nor society as God intends exist merely to provide humans with entertainment and escape from reality.

Rather, all the world is a habitat, large enough and diverse enough to support all that life can do and be.

Once we learn to see and admire what life is doing and how life does it, we lose our taste for staged performances and come to view them with valid suspicion.

God never ceded sovereignty over the planet to humans to use as they see fit. Neither have we.

All the world is God's workshop to be used for God's creative purposes.

Day 82

If there are no stages with large gathered, eagerly anticipating crowds, there will be no things done just for show and applause, praise, and profit.

Those who just want to be the constant center of attention in place of God will exclude themselves from what we are doing. That is for the best, because they are carriers of the most virulent form of the disease afflicting humanity.

Lacking any performance stages, what will be done will be done because it is true, effective, and necessary for life to move on toward God's purposes.

Day 83

We don't do our work on exalted stages because God will not meet us there.

We work around common tables where we can all see and hear each other. Here we can reason with each other while looking each other in eye. We can catch errors before they turn into decisions or habits.

Work done around a table followed by coordinated efforts away from the table is then evaluated and improved back at the table, or standing in a hallway.

"Table work" is teamwork. Teamwork in service of a larger value, in fulfillment of a shared calling fosters ethical regeneration in a way that nothing else can. Teamwork in the pursuit of truthful effectiveness honors God, the author of truthful effectiveness. When so honored, God meets us in such a setting in the form of ethical and practical clarity.

Day 84

The worktable is our only human-made sanctuary, the only place we gather as groups to meet the mind of God. Here every face can be seen as fully as the next one and every voice can be fully heard until understood.

Our personal sanctuary is nature, alone with God. Even there, especially there, we are part of our first and highest team, learning the best form of cooperation to which humans are called and of which humans are fully capable.

In neither the sanctuary of the worktable nor the sanctuary of solitude with God in nature can we hide who we really are and what we really want, unlike the staged performances we no longer trust. Exposed constantly to the wisdom of nature and scrutiny of our teammates our errors are exposed and corrected. As a result, we constantly become more fit for the work we are called to do. It is the way of life, already there to admire, emulate and join.

Day 85

The result of our work together is not a passing moment of adulation and applause for one star or a privileged few.

Rather, the result of our teamwork over time is a growing, inclusive diversity - a habitat in which many lives and many types of life thrive alongside each other, because of each other. Working together, we create something far better than applause. We create peace.

True peace opens the heart to God, and all God has in store. God made us to hear our calling in moments of peaceful silence, not in the roar of the crowd.

It is all a question of beginnings.

Our founding memories do not hearken back to any sermon on any mount by any religious celebrity, or to any speech on any platform by any political celebrity. Our founding memories are deeply personal, quiet, and intimate.

Each of us remembers vividly the moment when, surrounded by nature, we became aware that God is real, when with new eyes we saw that where God rules things work together in a state of living, beautiful peace.

Day 86

Peace is not the absence of tension; it is the creative management of natural and necessary tension between two or more truths about reality. Certain conditions are necessary to manage tension productively.

Once the worktable gets too big, it becomes an irresistible stage for attention-seeking performers, not a workstation for teammates. Beyond 8 or 9 people, it becomes almost impossible to be one team instead of several competing teams.

"Us" versus "them" statements signal a change in identity that leaves insiders and outsiders. Somehow we are not managing the tension between us as well as we could so that everyone feels they live inside the same identity, sharing the same concerns and aspirations.

We stop working on the project and work instead on the team. Somewhere along the way, one of us feels that giving and receiving timely helpful effort was not reciprocated, which is unjust. This cannot go unaddressed. We will bring no more justice to our world than we are able to bring to each other around the table.

We seek God in solitude, listen, wait, and respond to the correcting touch we receive. We return to the worktable and alter the way we have been treating each other when we do our work. This process keeps us flexible and adaptable.

Day 87

What is flexible and adaptable is sustainable.

What is rigid and reactive will cease to exist as it is leaped over and left behind by life.

At the beating heart of any human endeavor that remains receptive, responsive, flexible, creative, and adaptable is an honorable, ethical, high functioning team.

That is why, if you boil it down to its essence, *teamwork* is the only feature of our religion that is observable to others, not ceremonies and rituals. When working on a high-functioning team you can't hide your bad intent, faulty thinking, laziness, or incompetence. While putting on rituals and ceremonies you can hide all that harmful nonsense and more.

We make it clear in everything we do that others can see that thriving diversity is our goal, not the accumulation and display of fancy shiny stuff. Fancy shiny stuff cannot adapt to changes in the environment, only an ethically guided team can do that.

Day 88

Teamwork is a form of life. Life moves along cooperative pathways. There are natural pathways leading from God, the cause of life, out into the world. Each natural pathway leads to the next and builds on the one before it. The pathways are all open-ended and culminate in the open-endedness that characterizes all living systems.

Each pathway also leads back to God, as the wonders that unfold along each one can only be explained, sustained, and enhanced by following God's ethical direction.

Life pathways that lead to fitness endure; ones that don't lead to fitness die out. Fitness means the robust capacity to meet and solve the problems a creature faces in its changing environment. The biggest problems are so big no individual creature can solve them alone, they must be solved collectively – voluntarily, not through bribery or threats.

Forced cooperation creates only temporary, apparent, compliance, it does not create commitment, initiative, or innovation. Instead, forced cooperation sets up a backlash that will quickly undo everything forced cooperation built over generations.

Day 89

The voluntary cooperative pathways of life converge into a fitness that ensures the survival of a social species despite major changes in its environment. Cooperations ensures survival first by minimizing the dangers in those changes, and only then by optimizing the new opportunities presented by the changes.

God designed life strategies fit to first survive potential harm, and then to thrive. Unfit strategies are designed to do the opposite – to thrive as much, and as soon as possible, as the priority, leaving nothing useful in place to survive major losses.

Day 90

All of God's natural cooperative pathways are required to achieve the collective fitness needed to sustain sustainability. Each one makes the next one possible and fulfills the promise of the last one. Take any one of the pathways out and the path of life dwindles down to nothing. All the cooperative pathways are ethical at the core and practical at the surface. They are all about how we treat the other lives around us as we move to meet and solve the problems we face together.

In nature, none of the cooperative pathways are for show, or exist just to produce entertaining shows.

The world is not a stage after all. The world is a workshop in which The Creator calls forth, protects and guides a few human creations that are true to life through and beyond the many human creations that aren't true to life.

Day 91

A cooperative pathway is a pattern of mutually helpful, cooperative values, attitudes, behaviors and finally, choices. Where these virtues exist and complement each other there is a functioning, reliable base camp. Base camp is where those doing worthy work can go to rest, refuel and re-tool so they can re-engage the work refreshed and renewed.

Choices are especially important in a cooperative pathway. We arrive at critical moments when the choice we face is hard and costly. We can either enact a cooperative value that will cost us comfort and ease now but benefit many far into the future, or we can enact a selfish value that will benefit one or a few right now but make the future worse for everyone else.

With each costly choice, the base camp is renewed. With each selfish choice, the base camp is degraded, until finally it no longer exists in any reliable form.

Day 92

We will discuss the early cooperative pathways that are the most visible and immediately accessible. The later ones come into view when we stand on the earlier ones we have built into our lives, but there are hints where the later ones will most likely appear as needed.

The first cooperative pathway is the intimate, daily relationship between each of us individually and God, informed by the genius we see in how nature solves complex problems, overcomes challenges and copes with change.

If we stay intimately connected to God, in a regenerating state, it will be clear as it happens that the ethical choice is best. For those who live disconnected from God, it only becomes clear in hindsight that the ethical choice would have been the better one, at which point it is too late, the damage is already done.

Without this primary cooperative relationship with our Creator nothing we do will work out well because God alone is the original source of life's problem-solving genius.

Day 93

Cooperation is about forming alliances around a shared purpose.

Unlike our other cooperative relationships, our relationship with God carries with it access to unlimited knowledge, unlimited presence, and unlimited power.

We continue to seek alliance with the One who cannot lose, even after we have learned that sustained contact with God will require us to shed and leave behind anything that God does not endorse or support.

The tradeoff is well worth it. We lose dross to gain pure gold; we lose error to gain an ever more accurate understanding of reality. We lose the role of passive spectator to gain the role of active participant. We lose unhealthy dependence on what is not reliable to gain healthy, voluntary dependence upon One who never fails to meet us, teach us and help us do what we were created and called to do.

Day 94

God alone is all-knowing. God alone knows the cooperative pathways life will find to make its way through a future that is always changing and has not yet taken form.

To meet the future God has in store, we must be both individually and collectively...

Content, which is what it means to be happy.

Ever wiser, which is what it means to understand what knowledge we will and won't need, plus how to gain and use it.

Functionally complete, which is what it means to be holy.

(Whole-ness and holiness are the same thing.)

Day 95

Seeing the future that we can't see, God knows that stuff won't make us happy, that accumulating more information won't make us wise and that that ritual won't make us holy.

It is telling that accumulating stuff, observing a ritual, and learning more facts do not require ethical choices or intimate cooperation between equals. In fact, often no cooperative behavior is required at all because all these activities can be done at a safe distance from another life.

God directs us away from those false pathways and onto the cooperative pathways life will take into a currently unformed, emerging future.

It is in this new expansive space we will discover God has used our journey to fit us for life on life's terms.

Day 96

Everything is not equally important to sustain life. Paramedics have a priority system when it comes to saving lives – ABC. Airway, breathing, circulation. Before doing anything else, check if the patient is breathing and clear the airway if needed. Give rescue breaths if the patient isn't breathing. Perform chest compressions to restore blood circulation. In that order.

To create a sustainable civilization, we must first restore the breath of life, the living, active, daily, ethical presence of God in our lives. Without that everything else we do will die anyway.

Our first priority is to individually form and maintain our first and most important cooperative relationship - with our Creator. This is because our minds, once prepared by observing the patterns of divine genius in nature, are purpose-built to receive and respond creatively to daily, specific, situation-fitting guidance from God, alone, directly, in quiet solitude.

Day 97

We seek and receive gentle promptings each day from God to find and enter openings life will flow through into the future. Ultimately, we are not just seekers. We were created to be finders.

In nature, a creature that only and forever seeks, but never finds, will soon die.

We use imagination to anticipate and find openings that allow us to enter a deeper understanding of reality.

We don't use imagination to escape reality.

We don't use imagination to create something that replaces reality.

To misuse our God-given capacity for imagination to escape or replace what is real, material, observable, measurable and testable - is to put ourselves on a path chasing a mirage. When we get "there" we find nothing and slowly die trying to feed ourselves on illusions.

Day 98

We learn to spot the difference between a true opening and a false one.

There is no non-material, non-substantive world that we can access and then "manifest" into a tangible reality, by some secret magic technique.

There is no world of perfect forms, ideal models of which particular real objects are only flawed examples. There is only the material created universe of real things made from combining smaller real things.

Even ideas are held in neuropathways made of fibers coming off our nerve cells. The synapses that carry signals across gaps in the pathways, when strong enough, are themselves made of proteins, which are very real, observable, measurable building blocks of life.

Rather than dismissing physical realities and attempting to live untouched by them, we respect physical realities. We know things are as they are for reasons that don't just go away because we want them to.

An opening is when God meets us deeper inside reality, not outside of it. This is because there is no place outside physical reality for the meeting to occur.

Day 99

As we seek and follow God's ethical direction our attention is directed to the general area where God will eventually create openings before us. There is nothing about the opening that violates the laws of nature, but the occurrence is rare.

The opening will not be a way to get more things for us or our group, at the expense of other lives. The opening will be a practical way to add to the stock of happiness all creatures around us can draw upon.

Each opening in a situation and each passage through it into a deeper understanding of reality will be a uniquely given and guided event, never to be repeated. It is one of those things where "you just had to be there," ready, prepared, nimble, motivated and competently responsive.

Openings are "before and after" events in our lives, both individually and collectively. Life paths that come from God are built out of on-going, "eventuated" processes, producing outcomes that were completely dependent upon unforeseen events we did not cause, but we were led to spot and optimize.

Day 100

What was possible to do before an opening event given by God, is wholly different from what will be possible to do after the opening event. The new possibilities we can now make real in the world will not be copies or mere extensions of anything that existed before.

After any God-created event we find a new surprise. We can create a qualitatively different combination of new insights and behaviors that create a larger, more inclusive, healthier, more diverse community of life. God's events always open into a broader field of justice for all. Anything else or less is an illusion and it is not from God. We learn to tell the difference and move on.

God's events, when we enter them under ethical guidance, make the life of the average person better, whereas ungodly work makes life better only for the privileged few at the expense of everyone and everything else.

Day 101

These situation-transforming events cannot be predicted, so they cannot be mass-produced, canned, and distributed by any human organization.

Yet, once they occur the new, different, and better combination of behaviors we create can be built upon, improved and extended by ordinary people with ordinary abilities, using common sense, persistence, and hard work.

Our civilization is an inclusive meritocracy. Doomed civilizations, by contrast, restrict opportunities to members of the club, so they can hoard all the gains for themselves and their offspring.

A path made possible by unforeseen events can only be optimized by individuals who live in private contact with God and then work in teams of individuals who also live the same way. Anyone can do this, no matter what their background.

We can start anywhere, at any time, with what we find at hand in our situation. Daily, we can seek and follow God. When we face a problem our impulse is not to seek a product to buy or a guru to follow. We don't seek a soothing and ecstatic experience, whether drug induced or theatrically produced. We don't seek to find out what the herd is thinking to know that to think ourselves. We often don't know what to do, but we always know who does.

Day 102

When we face a problem we're not sure how to solve ethically, seek God. Not a someone who claims to represent God, or a contrived representation of God. We seek God, alone, personally, in nature if at all possible.

Seeking God first and constantly is what makes us different in a way that makes all the difference. As long as we keep seeking God we find we are led through and out of any wasteland.

We find just enough of whatever we need, just in time, to continue the journey and meet the practical needs of the day, while harming no one who has nothing to harm us. We don't consider being different from us to be the same as harming us.

God delights in differences.

Day 103

Staying connected to God; we find ourselves guided through each critical decision we face as we encounter the complexities of each new situation we face. Our guided actions put us into a new situation we have not faced before, requiring new decisions yet again.

And again. And again. This is the way life is designed to evolve itself.

God will be with us through every unfolding of life as long as we see being with God as the highest state of human existence.

We do not envy or pine for anything else as if it is better, because there is no such thing.

Day 104

With each team member constantly receiving ethical correction from God, a problem-solving team can struggle productively with their differences to surmount the challenges they find in their local, immediate situation.

To the amazement of the working team, they enter together into a state of happiness that is higher and sturdier than any happiness resulting from any accumulation of stuff or pleasurable experiences. The team experiences a happiness that cannot leave us jaded, because it is ever new and surprising, leaving them ever more open to the unfolding wonders of God's creative genius.

Day 105

A godly team finds that the living wholeness and health growing between them is more enjoyable than the temporary mood elevation that comes from performative rituals or the smug superiority that comes from academic constructs.

They find they naturally want to be kind and generous with each other – the true mark of growing wisdom in an individual and group.

It makes sense. None of us want to harm a relationship we will likely need to access again in the future. But it is more than that. Our natural cooperation is a thing of delicate beauty. No healthy person wants to damage something delicate and beautiful, making their own world uglier.

Day 106

A godly team finds the work they produce is useful, simple, and elegantly beautiful, with little if any waste.

They find they have no need or desire to advertise what they do or how they do it. Their reputation precedes them. Through word-of-mouth others looking for something better are drawn to the unique quality of the team's work. Even more so, worthy, and ready minds are drawn to how the team works together to consistently create better solutions.

Those who value functionality and natural beauty, who want to see both high organization and high diversity, find their way after a long search, to the place where such things are normal. They arrive ready to learn, prepared by the journey itself, by experiencing the hollowness of everything else. By process of elimination, they know first-hand, that there is something very special going on in the workshops where God rules.

Day 107

Natural cooperative life paths have a defining trait: newness.

There is a surprising, satisfying freshness as life unfolds. Think about a wonderful new piece of music when you hear it for the first time. Each note is fresh and surprising, and yet somehow inevitable. After you hear the note in its place in the composition, you feel it could not have been different and could not have been better.

It is the same experience with any work touched by divine genius.

Or think about the fresh smell of a forest, meadow of beach. The fresh, enlivening smell announces the presence of thriving life, even in the dark or around a corner. Next to touch, smell is probably the most reliable sense we have - telling us something good or something bad is nearby.

Day 108

Unnatural life paths that lead to extinction have a defining trait as well: sameness. The only change is more - just more of the same. Cancers never stop growing and on their own, they only get bigger. More of the same is the path of cancer. It uses the processes of life against its own host.

It has been said that tradition is the dictatorship of dead people, and a popular fad is the dictatorship of living people. In both cases the defining feature is mindless, situation-blind imitation of what already was in place or currently is in place. In both cases people act as if they were robots running on mass-produced software.

In the case of tradition, the behavior is the same as it was years ago, even though our situation has changed. Such out-of-sync rigidity does not appear in natural systems.

In the case of popular fads, the behavior is the same everywhere, even though one's personal, local situation is different from the situation of the one who invented the fad. Such numbing monotony does not appear in natural systems.

Day 109

Sameness also gives off a smell: staleness or even a stench.

Dead tradition smells damp and stale.

Popular fads give off the stench of self-praise, designed to get attention and arouse envy.

We just follow our noses and keep moving – away from what stinks and toward what is fresh, new, surprising, and alive.

Day 110

In God's design life creates *more* by creating more varieties of life. Life specializes in the surprisingly new and different, not in just producing more of the same. Trusting and following more of the same is worshiping something created by a limited mind instead of the mind of the Unlimited Creator. It is to live apart from Creation instead of living as part of Creation. Not at first, but eventually It becomes deadly dull. It is possible to die of boredom, at least on the inside.

A path that prioritizes stuff, rituals, the latest popular knowledge, and techniques, all mass-produced, canned and distributed, is a path of waste that ends in extinction.

A path that prioritizes direct and cooperative relationships, empathy, ethics, real contact with our own local situation, keen perception, first-hand learning, exploration, and experimentation, is a path of elegant efficiency that leads to ever-evolving, ever-unfolding life.

Day 111

We don't worry that we're just reinventing the wheel. Nothing has been more constantly reinvented and improved than the wheel. None of us would want to go anywhere on the crude wheels humans first invented. None of those wheels would survive the speeds, torque and loads wheels must endure today anyway.

It is no more practical or enjoyable to live inside old religious ideas. They just can't bear the load, handle the speed, or absorb the torque of what humanity has become, given all the new information we have about how nature works.

The original core idea had two ideas with merit: there is a greater intelligence than our own, and we can interact with that intelligence in some way. So far so good. From there it got silly. The next idea was that humans could use gimmicks to make that greater intelligence do our bidding, as if we know best. Nonsense!

Time to reinvent that third idea so the whole thing rolls without ending up in the ditch of extinction. Time to discover and demonstrate the right relationship to the greater mind, the One who does know best.

Time to set the record straight.

Day 112

Many old silly religious notions put us in conflict with nature. Even when they didn't do that they pitted us against each other. Either way we were traveling down paths to death.

True life-paths come from God and lead back to God. They are marked by long, sustained effort, rational risk-taking, and experiments. Some of our experiments fail because we don't' yet understand reality well enough.

We acknowledge and learn from our failures so we can learn to do something new, different, and better. The reason the experiment failed often holds the key to unlocking a mystery, pregnant with creative possibility.

We accept the loss but find and retain its lessons. Most of all, we retain and grow our curiosity and sense of adventure. We return to the work and start again, with a deeper understanding of what we are doing.

Day 113

Any path life takes into the future will be new every morning, in at least some small way, if we pay close attention to what is happening around and between us.

Our path is forever interesting, but it is not a path for the lazy, the cowardly, or the vain. We learn it is counterproductive to enlist them as traveling partners.

The lazy won't do the work. The cowardly won't take any risk, no matter how necessary it is to learn the real reasons something does or doesn't work. The vain cannot acknowledge error or failure because they maintain an image of certain perfection to control and then exploit the efforts of others, while doing no serious work themselves.

Day 114

Something wonderful comes along with a path of newness: youth. We are always at the beginning of a developmental process, which makes us feel young inside, even as we accept the natural limitations that come with age. We tend to be old souls when we are young, because we can sense things are not right with a civilization guided and governed by unlimited selfishness.

But by staying close and faithful to God, we tend to be young souls when we are old, as all that God has directed us to learn and do starts to combine and ripen into a life and work of unique usefulness. We find that what we felt called to do in our youth, we are finally able to do in our mature years.

Those who do not seek closeness with God have the opposite experience. They are young and full of hope when they are young, then old and cynical when they are old.

Day 115

Our happiness was always different, and it really shows in our later years. There is a different look in our eyes and expression on our faces that cannot be faked, because it shows up most vividly in our unplanned reactions to the things that happen around us – both good and bad. We instantly set about to make the bad less bad and to find any good possibilities in it – with little or no energy wasted complaining. And now we know just how to do that. In our youth we didn't and couldn't.

We instantly set about making the good even better, to distribute widely and freely, with no energy spent trying to get attention and praise for doing so. And we know just how to do that. In our youth we didn't and couldn't.

Day 116

Those on a godless, lifeless path have good reasons to bemoan getting older, because they have nothing to look forward to but death.

By contrast, we see in the observable, verifiable results of our actions good reasons to rejoice in the fruits of hard-earned, applied wisdom.

Because we have lived a life of listening-obedience, we can realistically look forward to our offspring and our work moving fruitfully into the future. We don't need to use hollow internal cheerleading sessions to encourage ourselves. We can use facts and logic to project that a better future is now possible, and more likely to happen, because of what we put in motion over the course of our lives.

Day 117

We can connect the beginning of our journey and the end of our journey, because keeping the promises we made to God in our youth and fulfilling the calling we felt in our youth, has put in place a solid, new beginning other people can build upon, using their unique gifts and experiences.

We did not spend our lives following the herd or chasing fads. It was a lonely path, but we chose not to build a house of cards. We built a community of life.

The more closely one examines what we created together with those on our team, the more admiration one feels. The more one relies upon our work, the more gratitude one feels.

Day 118

An acorn can become an oak, but an oak cannot become an acorn again – which is what the godless long to do.

On the other hand, a mature, healthy, weather-beaten oak can produce acorns, by the thousands and the cycle of life goes on.

A godly life always leaves a legacy of sturdy excellence which others can build upon, not bitter disappointment, pining for the past.

Day 119

After we learn to be on God's team, under God's supervision, the next natural path of life is to protect and cultivate the full potential of those most closely related to us genetically. Those who share our genetics share some traits with us.

A trait is a behavior that is not learned and can't be taught, it can only be nurtured and cultivated. All it takes to activate a trait is to see it being used by someone else. A trait shows up consistently and predictably across all parts of our lives. It is not a situation-dependent tactic that we use when it is advantageous and forget when it is not. A trait won't go away and won't leave us alone. A trait speaks to us without words, often in our dreams, from deep inside. A trait directs us away from some activities toward others.

Day 120

As a trait expresses itself it may put us at odds with others who don't share the trait, and with the times and culture within which we find ourselves. Only someone who shares the trait can really understand what we're going through and help us minimize the downside and optimize the upside of having the trait.

Others who don't share the trait will often see it as a flaw that should be removed and will say so. Only one who shares our trait can assure us it is a gift from God, that it means there is something right with us, not something wrong with us. But we do need to learn how to manage it, while respecting it.

Day 121

Genetics gives us a trait which our then environment either suppresses or encourages. The more rare, fine, and valuable the trait is for a social species, the more dramatic will be the impact of either bad or good treatment on one who has the trait.

If the trait is suppressed and punished the loss to the individual and to society at large is enormous and often irreparable.

If the trait is honored and nurtured the individual thrives. The individual's work flourishes and bears fruit. Eventually the society around the individual will become healthier and happier.

Day 122

After learning to stay connected to God and nature, our second duty, our second highest calling, is the protection and care of those most closely related to us. It is our duty to forge an effective working team with them if at all possible.

We never abandon or skip over this primary, natural responsibility in a rush to bring something into the world that claims to make a difference.

The vain need to go out in public or far away to someplace exotic to prove how righteous they are. Any movement that started with a clever, charismatic person abandoning kin and seeking immediate public attention, is not from God. That is not the way life has ever started something new and better that went on to replace something outlived and useless.

Day 123

The godly see it as natural, necessary, and rewarding to take good care of the other lives they know most intimately. These are the same people who know them most intimately and will know whether their behavior is ethical, reciprocal, genuine and useful, or not. These are the people God has already placed in their lives through natural biological processes.

Just as migrating birds undertake long, arduous and dangerous journeys for the sake of their offspring, we too spare no effort, no expense, and manage any peril to enact our innate drive to participate in life by seeing to it that our own kin can have the life God intended for them.

It is the way of life. Life already knows best. Confused and misguided by millennia of godless culture, we humans are the late comers who need to play catch up.

Day 124

The drive to participate in life on life's terms means we naturally want to pass on and enhance what was given to us by God. Those of us who were given great talents and enriching experiences have more to pass on and enhance. Our opportunity is greater, so we make the most of our traits and the traits of those we are most intimately connected to. Enhancing the experience of our closest kin is uniquely rewarding because we can feel that they are somehow in us and we are somehow in them. To enhance their lives is to enhance and expand our own.

- We "get each other" in a way no one else can, so we can give to each other in a way that no one else can. It doesn't matter whether or not someone related to us ever gave to us in this way, even if we wish they had. What matters is that we do so now that it is our turn to choose.

Day 125

One technical definition of "duty" is the unit of work done for each unit of fuel an engine uses up. We are here to be engines of life and catalysts of justice. The unit of fuel we have been supplied is our time of conscious tenancy on earth.

We perform our duty to participate in life in the dash that will appear in our obituary between the year of our birth and the year of our death.

Anything that happened in that time gap that harmed or neglected those who share traits with us will take away from what could have been created if we had not behaved that way.

Nothing grieves God more.

Anything that we do in that time gap that helps and supports the growth of those who share our traits will release and multiply what can be, unleashing the full creative potential of what God already put in place.

Nothing delights God more.

Day 126

In nature, among social species, the training process is reciprocal. The trainer is trained as much or more than the trainee, learning by trial and error.

When we help develop someone who shares a trait with us, we immediately recognize what is happening when they get stuck and frustrated in a way that someone else could not. All real, lasting, effective education is done one-on-one.

One-to-group education, can at best, provide some background information, but it cannot convey real wisdom, tacit knowledge, and situational mastery.

Day 127

In a one-to-one setting, with no one watching, we can pay close attention, long enough, until we can do just the right thing, in just the right way, at just the right time, to help one unique individual.

No commercial entity, no non-profit organization, no government agency can provide this kind of precisely timed and fitted service. Only life can, doing what it does the way it naturally does it.

Our struggling kin must do the work themselves, but when we provide just the right insight, when they need it to get unstuck and growing again, they can keep moving toward full maturity. We help them locate and use something they already have inside but are not using at all or using effectively.

Because we love them so deeply without even choosing to, we naturally want to do this trait activation and cultivation work, even though it is messy, hard, and takes years to bear fruit.

Day 128

When we are helping our kin optimize a shared trait, we are willing to take the risk of having our guidance rejected, which often happens for quite some time. Love alone can bear the pain of having a gift go unvalued and unused. Love can stand watch and wait until God creates an opening event in the life of our kin that changes everything.

Love can wait decades if necessary to be helpful.

In contrast, unregenerate selfishness cannot wait to be rewarded with praise and profit. It resents and neglects kin responsibilities. The vain rush out to find an audience of fawning, uncritical strangers as soon as possible, the bigger the better. Vanity then puts on a show and charges admission in some form.

Day 129

Our most potent traits give us the most trouble, initially. Only our Creator can train us to manage them constructively over time, using feedback loops of trial and error.

Once we have learned how to make the most of our own most potent traits, we are uniquely suited to help those who share the same traits. This intimate training process is motivated and carefully guided by the deepest human love one can experience.

The love flows in both directions, as we learn the most from those we love the most. Those we love the most are those we trust the most because we know from direct and continuous contact that they truly want what is best for us.

Day 130

There are issues we know how to manage successfully and do so on a regular basis without nasty surprises. Our knowledge and skills are enough to guide us. These are generally pretty small and routine matters. The stakes are also small. Any loss we may incur by making a mistake we can recover from and know how to do so.

There are issues that are so vast and cover such vast time scales that we don't even attempt to manage them. For example, our sun will eventually die and in the process consume the earth, but we don't spend time worrying about that. The stakes are huge but won't play out in our own lifetimes.

Then there are issues that lie in the middle. We don't know how they will work out, but they lie within the time frame of our own lives or the lives of our loved ones. How they turn out matters. The stakes are very high. Yes, there is too much uncertainty to know how any particular approach will turn out in time. We find ourselves enveloped in ambiguity. Ambiguity causes anxiety.

Anxiety is natural and is a gift from God. Anxiety prompts us to stop, seek God and ask for wisdom and guidance. When we finally have reached the limit of our own certainty we have finally reached the threshold of God's direct involvement in our lives.

Day 131

When we come to a zone of uncertainty, we shouldn't expect quick or easy answers. The larger the issue and the more complex it is, the longer it will take to understand what is really going on. We fall silent and listen. We use all our senses to better understand the realities of the situation we face. The right hemisphere of our brains starts to take the lead because it was built to deal with the new, changing, and ambiguous.

An issue with high stakes is one we can't deny or avoid without negative consequences. It must be addressed to move forward with our lives and to take care of those we love. It lies on our life path, often acting as a barrier. At these moments, our choices will either move us closer to God or farther way.

Day 132

Historically, when humans have faced ambiguity they have not sought God. Instead, they have sought anything and everything but God. They sought magical power to fill the gap between certain and uncertain future outcomes.

Magic is the attempt to coerce God to give us what we want on the other side of the barrier, which presumes we know best what we will need in the future. The only problem is how to manipulate God to intervene the way we want. This mechanical, transactional attitude toward God is insulting to God. As long as anyone has this attitude, God will be silent and absent in their lives.

Day 133

The absence of God in a life or in a society leaves a terrible vacuum that draws in all kinds of madness. In the absence of God's presence all kinds of cunning entities rush in and claim to the provide the meaning, belonging, direction, and hope that only God can provide.

We don't seek magical solutions to get what we think is best - because we know we can't know what is best to want in the first place.

We know who does know what is best, so we seek God in solitude. In quietness, informed by how nature solves problems and meets needs, we learn how to live and grow in a sustainable way.

Day 134

Without potassium plants cannot turn sunlight into sugar through photosynthesis. There is no substitute for potassium. It is either present, or it is not. This is a normal feature found in nature in many different forms. In complex, living systems there is one component that is more essential than all the others combined for which there is no substitute. Without it the rest of the system's capacities come to nothing.

In the middle zone, between certainty and uncertainty, the critical missing component is not clever magic, or aggressive force. Rather the critical component is robust teamwork, which itself has an essential component.

Day 135

The essential ingredient of robust teamwork is ethics. You can build ethics on truth. You can't build ethics on a factual error or an intentional lie, no matter how clever it is. Truth is humbling because it tells us we have limits that will never go away. Error is often an incomplete understanding that we act upon as if it were. Flattery is often what we want to be true because it tells us there is a way to live without limits.

Ethics, informed by a realistic understanding of the cause-and-effect dynamic in all relationships, will create firm boundaries around our choices and behaviors. Ethics limit our individual selfishness enough for us to participate in life on life's terms. Ethics allows us to be cooperative, to reciprocate fully when we are helped by others. Ethics limits the solutions we attempt as a team to those that do not harm the innocent or exclude those who are different.

Ethics makes us reliable to others and useful to God. Neither magic nor force require ethics. Those who try to manipulate God to get what they want inevitably try to manipulate others to get what they want. They will try to take as much as possible and give nothing but empty words and showy rituals in return, just as they do with God.

Day 136

For a social species, any pathway life takes into the future will require willing and timely cooperation. Just as a vacuum will suck in dirt and debris, any attitude or behavior that prevents willing cooperation when we are trying to find an ethical solution to an ambiguous situation, will draw in harmful solutions instead.

Harmful solutions to the ambiguity inherent in life form the foundations of all the doomed civilizations that have gone before us. To legitimize and make permanent unjust and harmful ways to deal with life's ambiguity, civilizations invent fantastic stories about gods, creation, being, and famous founders. None of the stories can be observed today or proven – but most of them can be disproven.

Day 137

Members of doomed, unsustainable societies are taught to turn off their senses and brains in order to accept nonsense as the founding charter of their society's religious, economic, and political institutions.

This is a very dangerous development. If a society can convince its members to believe absurd nonsense, then it can convince them to ignore or actively support organized atrocities it claims are unfortunate, but necessary to maintain the society's growing wealth and power.

The argument is that since bizarre and cruel behavior was necessary for their god or their heroes to get things started in the first place, from time to time it is necessary for a society to do bizarre and cruel things to sustain and glorify itself.

This madness is both the root cause and description of an unsustainable social order. When scholars and scientists use facts and logic to finally disprove the founding stories of a civilization, it calls into question all the certainties built upon them. What collapses first in a doomed civilization is its system of certainties. Afterwards, the next generation has no compelling reason to help maintain a cruel fraud.

Day 138

We leave behind cruel and ludicrous myths and follow the cooperative wisdom already embedded in life itself.

Life's successful passage through any ambiguous, changing situation will be guided by the same intelligence that created life in the first place. God's happiness catches up to us, meets us, and fills us, precisely as we enter life's ambiguity with the determination to behave ethically. This is true on both the individual and collective level.

In the timely meeting of the divine and human mind there are new and better solutions which we could not have imagined before. Finding these solutions and working them out satisfies much of longing for meaning we feel.

Day 139

God meets us, touches our hearts, teaches our minds, provides timely help, and creates unforeseen openings - only on an ethical path. We enter and help expand a field of more life, more justice, more messy inclusion, more conflict, and conflict resolution, to create more tensed diversity – and with it more possibilities for original, creative combinations. The whole process never ends and is not easy. But it sure is worth it! On this creative journey with God, we feel alive.

We are filled with meaning that is not attached to any visible passing human invention, but to something invisible that cannot ever go away because it is eternal. We attach our will to live to what was there before anything was created and will be there after everything is gone.

Day 140

The will to live gives a reason to get out of bed in the morning and face the day. The will to live must have an anchor that is invisible because everything visible changes and eventually succumbs to entropy. If we anchor our willingness to keep living in something that vanishes, then when it vanishes, it will take our will to live with it. When we lose our will to live we enter a type of living death, like a zombie.

Historically, suicides and other deaths of despair increase, especially among men, when a people no longer believe there is goodness and wisdom in the way their society does things. Despair in a growing number of individuals is the leading indicator that a society is headed down an unsustainable path. Its leaders may get rich, more powerful, and more famous – but everyone else must get up each day and face a dwindling future.

Day 141

Life already has a way and is underway using it. We learn life's way and follow by staying within the ethical limits God has set for us.

By living this way, we will have helped create around us, in our own small local situation, a society in which it is normal to participate in life by cooperating and helping each other. For us it will feel familiar and natural to work together through a crisis none of us can surmount on our own, making sure all of us get through it safely.

In our company, dying souls come back to life and find life is worth living. The living touch of personal kindness is the only power that can raise the dead.

Day 142

We have learned by experience God does not meet us, teach us, or help us on an unethical path. Anytime we believe we must lie, harm someone and take without reciprocating to get where we want to go something is wrong with our sense of direction. When we believe we must do to others what we don't want anyone to do to us we have believed a lie. When we think we can't keep what we have, or we can't stay on schedule with our plans unless we trample the hopes of others, we are hallucinating.. We are seeing something that is not there.

When deliberately choose to see what is there by ignoring the pain and loss we cause when we act on these selfish impulses we leave the path of life. When we think we know better than God and act on that belief, we move onto an unsustainable path to death. We will live through the slow painful disintegration of everything we spent our lives building.

Every time we act unethically we help create a society in which it is normal to reject cooperating with each other. This leaves us paralyzed when a crisis occurs that can only be surmounted by working together willingly. Everything we gained by tricking or coercing others will be lost in a crisis that sets everyone against everyone. The gain is not worth the loss.

Day 143

The peace that comes from justice is what turns the predictive promise of truth into a living reality that can be observed.

In contrast, on a godless path, eventually the only way to turn the predictive promise of lies into lived reality is to use trickery, then force, then violence, and finally terror.

There is nothing more important than what we do with our attention when we face a frightening, ambiguous situation whose outcome we can neither predict nor control. The moment of ambiguity is the moment of truth. What we really believe to be true is what we will cling to and enact in that moment.

Day 144

In the moment of truth, anything we choose to do that prevents us from turning our attention to God and keeping it there will also function to direct our attention away from God and onto something that claims to be as good or better than God.

There is no such thing. It is a mirage. Lies that promise a life without limits only serve to direct our attention to an abyss of nothingness where all we find is the despair of broken promises.

Day 145

The way we chose to behave when we face an ambiguous situation invites the rule of God into our hearts and into our midst as a group. God enters and governs each heart directly, with no human or human institution acting as go-between. We cultivate the part of our brain that is curious, open, non-judgmental, and flexible. This trusting, child-like part of our brain is the access point for God's guiding presence.

As we meet to address our ambiguous situation together, after having each sought God alone in openness and solitude, we find we see things differently. We also see things we didn't see before that were there all along.

Day 146

When we attempt to cooperate with each other to solve a problem, we don't immediately or easily agree. This too is from God.

We work to really listen to each other with the same attitude of quiet, trusting openness we have toward our Creator when enveloped in nature. We learn with and from each other until we have a more complete understanding of what we are facing, how it is changing, and what ethical options we have at our disposal.

We avoid unnecessary silly conflicts. However, cooperation does not come from avoiding all conflict. Skillful, confident, resilient cooperation is forged in the furnace of necessary conflict, when our significant viewpoints and interests are not the same.

God meets us in our conflicts as long as we manage them ethically. The solutions we arrive at in this way are new, unexpected, and naturally more sustainable. A novel synthesis arises when we take into account as many variables in our situation as time allows. Any one of those variables, if omitted from our consideration, could cause our solution to fail altogether or even cause more and bigger problems than it was designed to solve in the first place.

Day 147

When we face a high stakes, ambiguous situation, we gather and reason together. We then scatter to gather more information to fill in the gaps where at present we can only guess what is going on. We never move forward using guesswork alone. We replace guesswork with verifiable facts.

We draw ourselves together into a learning team. Paradoxically, the tension between our points of view, our divergent experiences and training is what draws us closer to each other, the same way both ends of a violin are pulled closer to each other through the tension of the string.

Day 148

As we become a learning team, the pull we feel toward each other comes from hearing a legitimate, logical, factual challenge to our original opinion. This is good. Opinions are different from facts, but we often confuse opinions with facts.

We may feel annoyed that our opinion was not immediately accepted as fact. We feel challenged. We answer the challenge with our own direct verifiable observations and logical arguments. This process of tense and protracted disagreement pulls us all more deeply into a shared understanding of our situation.

When engineers gather to solve a complex problem together they call this process "engineering tennis." It is a kind of disciplined play in which each engineer is hard on the problem but soft on the person who disagrees, always treating them as an esteemed colleague.

Just as the tennis racket would not work without the tension in its strings, the solution would not emergence without the motivated tension within and between the members of a learning team. No tension, no dynamic movement back and forth, no better new combination of ideas and methods to solve the challenge presented by a high stakes, ambiguous situation.

Day 149

The human mind is uniquely designed for communion with God, for admiring and learning from nature, and then for collaboration with each other using language, symbols, and tools like mathematics.

We don't invite God into our problem-solving and decision making through eloquent public prayers designed to show off our earnest righteousness.

We invite God into our midst by:

Treating God as infinitely beyond our understanding and control

Treating our natural environment with deep, careful respect as the source of models that inspire better, more elegant, and sustainable solutions.

Treating each other ethically

In this only in this mode of behavior that humans approach the sublime – the threshold of the Creator's workshop.

Day 150

In God's workshop alone what was once impossible becomes possible. Under the guidance, and correction of God's infinite mind there is no problem humanity faces that cannot be solved. God already knows the way around or through the challenges we face. God's omniscience will guide us by intimate touch, through a quiet voice, informed by the peaceful genius already embedded in nature. The solutions we find will be completely unlike the ones we have been using, utterly unforeseen and made possible only by events we can't predict or control.

In God's workshop situations reverse from hopelessness to joyful possibility, which, in time, can be worked into flourishing diverse fruitfulness. We live off the increase and share it widely. We created it together, so we share in its bounty together, and protect it as something forever held in common.

Living in this mode of learning, adjusting, creative teamwork, we fulfill our own individual destiny, the destiny of the group we belong to, finally we fulfill the destiny of humanity. It becomes vividly clear why we are here.

Day 151

An ethical creative team is sustained by our daily choices, especially when under stress.

If we choose to stop treating each other ethically, helpfully, and cooperatively,

If we refuse to do the work required to resolve our conflicts,

We won't create and maintain mutually beneficial, reciprocal relationships.

This leaves our efforts completely devoid of the guiding, enlivening presence of God. No more good surprises, only bad ones followed by ones that are even worse.

Entering an abyss of cynical hopelessness, we will soon see no point in human existence, and we will be right.

Living apart from God and creation can only end in bitter emptiness.

Day 152

Why would a member of an ethical creative team stop choosing to do what cooperation requires?

Apparent incentives.

Cultures that banish God's presence through systemic injustice offer seemingly endless pleasures as a substitute and distraction – for those who can afford them. Yet no pleasure can take the place of joy.

The problem is that no combination of pleasures can replace peace. No purchased product or service can match the feeling of being truly known, valued, and loved for who God created us to become.

We take a pass on pursuing every possible sensual pleasure or ecstatic experience. We don't see wallowing in pleasure as the fulfillment of human destiny because we know that in time it is all just more of the same and there is no lasting joy in it. And on the way, we know we would find it necessary to neglect or harm another life.

It just isn't worth it.

Day 153

The way we know we have stumbled onto a death path is we find ourselves torn up inside, divided against ourselves, and we find each other repulsive to be around.

We may feel there is something wrong with us that prevents us from having all the pleasures promised on this path. Others weren't born with the flaw we have and that is why they are enjoying all the pleasures, while we aren't. We may feel what we must do to be happy is not what we have the capacity and resources to do. It isn't fair. God got it wrong.

Or we may feel torn between what we want to do and what we know we ought to do, between our interests and our values. The part of our brain that is open, curious, creative, and flexible, is the part of ourselves that suffers the most pain when we are pitted against ourselves or each other. In this divided state the part of our brains that was made to know God and commune with nature will not let us sleep or sleep deeply enough to feel refreshed.

Day 154

All human evil is committed in this torn-up state of mind, not in a unified state of mind. A torn-up state of mind is very painful and causes anger, resentment, envy, anxiety and finally despair. In this painful state of mind many humans turn on themselves because they see themselves as the problem; while others turn on those around them, seeing those who are different or disagree as the problem.

The culture promised that being completely self-actualized would be wonderful. It turns out that completely self-actualized people are so completely selfish they are incapable of cooperating with each other.

One person who self-actualizes and creates a life with no ethical correction from God, who follows no patterns found in nature will inevitably find his or her plans frustrated or blocked by someone else doing the same thing the same way. Only the Creator can integrate our callings into a peaceful, productive whole. This is as true for nations as it is for individuals.

Day 155

Those who did not seek God to put them back together on the inside and who don't seek God's guidance as they build relationships find themselves unable to resolve both their inner and outer conflicts. When their goals conflict, godless worldings have nothing inside that can stop them from doing harm to those who get in the way. Despite their lofty promises to do good in the world, they do evil. They are so busy doing good they don't have time to be good.

Only godly earthlings can live up to their highest ideals by managing differences between them with courageous creativity.

Day 156

In contrast to what happens to those living on a godless path, those of us following a natural life path, given and guided by God, come to realize that how we were made is a good fit for the role we have been called to play. Even our losses were necessary to fit us to our calling.

We find what we actually need to do in our situation is what we have the capacity and resources to do. We are not mismatched to our calling. We find we need far less capacity than we thought we would need, but our capacity must function at a far higher level of precision and complexity.

We rise to a higher level of precise complexity as God teaches and trains us, using the realities of our situation as feedback-rich curriculum.

We find our values become our goals, so we don't' need to choose between them. This happens because our goals change. Our goal now is to stay close to God, to be useful and available for whatever needs doing. We bring everything confusing and concerning to God, who steers us ethically and practically. When it would be unethical to run away or do nothing, God guides our choices step by step, into and through whatever we face that initially confuses and concerns us.

Day 157

If since our youth we have sought God, admired and imitated nature, and sought to avoid the mistakes of history, the natural consequences of these unusual choices accumulate into a life that is unusual. We arrive in our later years internally unified, functionally complete and at peace with those in our lives, while making no claim to infallibility or flawlessness.

The completeness God brings about allows us to look back on our younger self with amazement at the strength it took to reject the fads of our youth.

Our younger self still lives inside us and can look at our mature self with admiration for finally coming to embody a working system of godly, natural values and virtues. We find we don't regret having paid the cost to follow God's ethical direction. Our only regrets are about the times we didn't. Unlike the godless, we didn't do it our way. We did it God's way which is life's way.

Day 158

We are grateful we have learned to wander off less and less from God's presence to chase popular fleeting illusions. We find we are now at our finest under pressure, when dealing with fluid, changing, ambiguous, high-stakes situations. Our decisions in these pivotal moments are sound and lead to true lasting good beyond what we could have imagined.

A true lasting good is one that naturally regulates, repairs, updates, and replaces itself as needed.

Only ethical teamwork can sustain truly good work through all the shocks and setbacks it will encounter as it makes its way through a constantly changing environment. Wherever we can establish ethical teamwork - either between us and another individual, or between our learning team and another learning team - we find God is with us in the effort. The discoveries we make together are worth the work and the wait.

Day 159

Ethical teamwork, starting with our closeness to God, helps us absorb shocks and quickly return to equilibrium emotionally and physically in the least amount of time possible.

In a car, shock absorbers keep the tires firmly in contact with the road where they can do their work of steering and braking.

If the ride is too cushy the tires are up in the air, not in contact with the road. The driver really can't feel what is happening to the car as it bounces up and down for way too long. The best thing to do is slow down and/or stay off rough roads altogether, even if such a road is the only one available, or to go really slow even if the need is urgent.

It is possible to feel so disconnected from reality that we under-react to problems when they appear. This is the monastic mode, a way of living we see nowhere in nature. It is not a life path.

On the other hand, if the ride is too stiff the driver feels every little bump constantly. He tires quickly, losing the attention necessary to pay attention to the road. The car will also shake itself to pieces, falling apart much faster than it needs to.

It is possible to react so constantly to small shocks that we have inadequate attention left to absorb and respond creatively to a significant moment of opportunity or danger. This is the mode of the haggling merchant, a way of living we see nowhere in nature. It is not a life path.

Day 160

A good team, working ethically, using spirited discussion, can accurately perceive what is happening in the situation and respond to it with precision and care.

It can also filter out what is a little thing that will likely resolve itself and doesn't require immediate attention.

Reacting to problems and opportunities appropriately as they arise is essential to sustain a long and challenging journey, because doing so keeps us firmly in touch with each other and with reality as it changes. For the most part, a protected, undistracted weekly check-in for a few hours is enough to maintain a good functioning team. During an acute crisis we call special meetings that may last a few days.

Day 161

Ethical teamwork is costly in terms of time and effort, but anything that prevents good teamwork will invite in a cheap substitute for good teamwork.

The lack of ethical teamwork will stop the development of all the good work a true team could have done. This vacuum of good results draws in all the bad outcomes that come with cheap substitutes.

Ethical teamwork is a good investment in terms of cost vs. benefit primarily because of all the suffering and loss it prevents.

Day 162

Life pathways are created by God and lie latent within our DNA. They represent different ways to access and exchange information and resources through healthy, on-going, voluntary relationships. God's pathways only start to open as we build up a history of mutual trust and reciprocity through repeated, direct interactions.

When we face a situation we don't know how to manage...

When we face a situation we can't manage alone....

The crucial question becomes – who are we going to call upon?

Who can we turn to?

Who will willingly run to our side, if needed?

Who will not mislead us, but will provide reliable information we can use?

Who will not neglect or abandon us, but will provide essential resources when needed?

If we can happily answer these questions we are happy people.

Day 163

Who can we reliably call on in our time of need?

The answer is – the same ones who know through long experience they can call upon us, our information, and resources. Those with whom we already have a healthy, voluntary relationship.

We can call upon those who know first-hand that we are competent and our information is reliable and who know from experience we will be by their side when needed. These are the same people who have good reason to believe we will take their side when their reputation is attacked, or their interests are threatened, especially in their absence, when it is needed most.

Day 164

Those who defend our reputation and interests when we aren't there to defend ourselves are those whose loyalty we have earned. They know we would do the same for them.

The list of people we know we can call upon who know they can call upon us includes those we encounter in the course of managing our normal, daily, practical activities. We don't need to go out and recruit members or collaborators. They show up naturally along the way.

Most often the path of natural, healthy cooperation starts with kin, then leads to friends and partners, then to neighbors and co-workers. From there, new paths open and branch out based on reputation.

Day 165

Word of mouth reputation tells us ahead of time what it will be like to interact with a person or group. Our reputation tells them ahead of time what to expect when they interact with us or our group.

The way life's elegant complexity grows among humans is we have heard good things about a person or working team. Another person or working team has heard good things about us. We can approach each other with reasonable confidence that we will find a way to create something between us that is more than the sum of the parts, something that creates a greater field of possibilities for both of us or both our groups.

With each new relationship we follow the same ethics we have learned from God. In so doing we invite God's creative genius into everything we do everywhere we go. Things just get better when we are around and that does not go unnoticed. We draw the best out of people. Our reputation precedes us.

Those who are already like us want to collaborate with us and those who are not like us will avoid us.

Day 166

God puts us on cooperative life pathways and keeps us there through constant course corrections. Course corrections are changes in our behavior that are both ethical and practical. It is our new, adjusted behaviors that keep us firmly in contact with reality as it changes beneath our feet.

God corrects our course when we are about to harm a relationship with those who have never harmed us, just so we can pursue something we imagine to be better than a network of mutual aid. We have learned there is no such thing as something better than a network of mutual aid so pursuing it is a path to surprised disappointment, grief and finally oblivion.

Day 167

God also corrects our course when we are about to do something that will only "work" short-term, but will set in motion big, unsolvable problems down the road. Often the way God does this it to prevent us from doing something we want to do. Only later do we realize God's prevention was an act of mercy, protecting us and our reputation from irreparable harm.

By contrast, when we accept God's preventions and make ethical and practical course corrections we build our reputations, earning the trust of those we may need to turn to someday in our own hour of need.

As we mature, we accept the fact that we are responsible to seek God's guidance before we act. Now, informed by years of experience, the way God most frequently prevents us from doing harm is to activate our conscience using a still small voice deep in our souls. We only hear when we slow down, become quiet, call out – and wait.

Day 168

Like water, life follows the shortest route possible to get where it is going. It does this by following the course of least resistance. Life does not require or even benefit from no resistance, but it will find the route where there is less resistance than there would be on any other available path.

Where will there be less resistance to the kind of healthy, mutual dependence we see in natural systems? Where there is a long-standing pattern of forming satisfying relationships that benefit all parties equally. Mighty rivers start as small, quiet trickles, and end large and wide, emptying into the ocean, completing their part of the ancient, global water cycle that sustains life on earth.

Our helpful relationships follow a similar pattern. Daily, quietly and in secret, we work to create a productive relationship with our Creator. The kind wisdom we learn there typically flows out first to touch our own kin, as we generally spend more time with them than anyone else. From there God's touch through our attitudes, values and behaviors flows to out the next most frequent contact to the next and so on.

Day 169

Like water following the course of least resistance, we find there is a sequence of relational experiences God uses to reactivate our natural cooperative instincts as a social species.

We learn to cooperate with a friend, with a life partner, with our offspring if we become parents.

We cultivate helpful relationships with neighbors.

As in nature, neighbors alert each other to a danger that threatens the neighborhood.

We build solid relationships with co-workers to get things done well, in sufficient quantity and on time. Any work unit functions at a higher level when we are there.

By the time we have learned how to behave in ways that make good, long-term relationships possible it feels completely normal to protect and grow those relationships.

By now we have built a reputation. Our reputation is like the reputation of a skilled gardener. People who have benefited from our competence know we can fix and grow things others can't.

Day 170

Our reputation opens doors to all kinds of other relationships, branching out in ways and directions we could never have foreseen. At each new opening, we enter with the same godly ethical behavior. We continue building trust and esteem carefully, ethically.

Courtesy, attention, and kindness combine to create an atmosphere in which people feel safe to learn and try new things. Life finds a way into the future that was not there before via the way we treat others,. Things start to happen that did not happen before we showed up and started behaving the way God has taught us to behave toward any creature.

Like a river, as life follows these relational paths it grows wider, deeper, and richer in diversity. One type of good relationship flows into and nourishes the next, the same way melting snow from one mountain peak joins with flows from other peaks, which join with larger flows from other valleys, and finally joins a great social river teeming with life. This is God's idea of civilization. We seek and accept nothing else and nothing less.

Day 171

The intimacy and creative richness found within each relational pathway is greater the earlier it appears in the sequence. The closer we are in proximity to another life and the more often we are in contact with that life, the more often we will use the relational pathway. The more often we use a relational pathway we can create more, more unique, and more useful solutions within the rich safety of the relationship.

Since God is in us, around us, in everything, above everything, beyond everything, existing before anything else existed, and existing after everything else is gone, then our most intimate, constant, and enveloping relationship is with God. It is in this primary relationship that the most unique and useful solutions (often re-solutions) first come to mind and there is an uninterrupted, daily flow of creative, practical, ethical adjustments to our real situation.

Day 172

What flows from intimacy with God is ever new and original because we spend our time with God working through how to respond to what happened yesterday and what we anticipate will happen today, all of which is novel, at least in its particulars. The divine is in the details.

What is stale, old, and predictable comes from something other than contact with God.

It is our relationship with God that we use constantly in every situation, and most intensely when managing our way through ambiguous, changing situations.

No matter what happens, with God we are never alone or unwatched. We are never unaccountable for our actions, but we are also never abandoned or forgotten in our situation.

Just as plants never stop seeking and relying on the sun, we never stop seeking and relying upon God first and most.

Day 173

Effective, productive, creative relationships are built by calling out for help and being answered, and by hearing another call out to us for help and answering the call quickly. We learn to add increasing precision and competence to our quick responses, to avoid making things worse.

Our relationship with God starts with God calling out to us. God calls out to us in solitude, in the quiet of our deepest self. God's callings are always calls for help. There is something God needs a human assistant to do. God helps those who have already been answering God's call for help not to get something in return, but simply because they love God and want God to be happy.

God's callings are quiet and calm, breaking through the noise of our concerns, worries and ambitions. God's callings meet us in our situation, no matter how messy it is. God's callings lead us up higher into a new situation that transcends and outlasts whatever situation we are in, no matter how distressing. We ascend in our situation by helping God immediately and constantly. We transcend beyond our situation when God helps us in the way, in the place at the time God sees fit. In that order.

We return to our daily situation with radiant faces, kinder, calmed, and focused, able to see what we couldn't see before and able to respond in ways we wouldn't have before.

Day 174

God calls out to us for the first time in our lives when we feel a sense of wonder at the beauty and order of nature. We come to realize we are dealing with a vast, infinite, intelligence, far beyond and superior to our own. We sense that nothing humans have ever made even begin to compare.

For most intractable problems it is the approach to the problem that is the problem. Missing this innate sense of which intelligence is vastly greater, it is impossible for humans to solve the problems of sustainability. With this sense of awed humility in place, humans can finally approach the work in the right way.

Day 175

The ability to recognize the presence of intelligence in a piece of work, and especially the presence of intelligence beyond one's own – is the surest evidence of high intelligence. High intelligence can sense there is purpose built into what one observes. High intelligence concludes that what is happening is not random. Rather, what is happening is necessary.

Healthy, natural systems embody complexity – the highly organized combination of a high number of lives that are very different from each other. Natural complexity is resilient – it is flexible and has a lot of back-up systems in it. If one fails, the other kicks in.

Humans have rarely achieved anything like a complexity that lives up to these standards. Yet God continually creates nothing but this kind of complexity.

High differentiation plus high organization is the signature of the divine, reminding us how much greater God is than we are.

Day 176

In nature there is never complexity for no reason. Complexity costs energy to build and maintain.

Because it is so costly, complexity in nature does not arise except to do something useful, something that would not happen without it. Complexity in nature is always functional and very often beautiful. What nature makes is irresistible, it appeals to our senses and arouses a strong desire to make something of our own lives that is just as appealing.

We know the complexity in nature is being caused somehow, even if the cause is not visible using our current methods of observation. The mystery of natural complexity calls out to souls that are not yet dead. It means nothing to those who died inside long ago, except as something to be used as a nice decoration.

Day 177

By hearing the calling of complexity, we sense God is working toward something beyond anything we can fully comprehend.

Observing the genius that is alive in nature teaches us to admire and trust God as the ultimate and final authority.

Only when we see God as the ultimate and final authority can we begin to relate to God in a functional and productive way. We trust we will be given more insight into what is going on when and if we need it to be useful to God and helpful to life.

Day 178

From observing nature, we learn admiration, humility, and gratitude. We learn to always give the benefit of the doubt to God. There is a reason the natural world is the way it is. We know it does something it was designed to do, even though we don't know precisely what that is.

A general sense that we are in the presence of great intelligence and a great, unfolding mystery is all we need. It is enough to keep our souls alive and growing, as pieces of the mystery become a bit clearer, daily.

We don't rely on elaborate theories about God to know God. Theories about God put us at a safe distance from God. This is not the experience we have in nature. There is an elevating effect on our attitudes and behaviors that comes as an unplanned, unsought, indirect effect when we stay in direct contact with God's intimate enveloping touch.

In contrast, human theologies most often create a smug self-righteousness that contrasts vividly with the humility and awe one feels around a naturalist. The reason is simple: you can learn everything about a human system of theology. You can never learn everything about creation because it is so vast and constantly evolving.

The essential thing we need to know about God is that God is the uncreated Creator. It will take a lifetime to even begin to unpack what that means. Anything more is a distraction that blocks contact with God and stops the ethical regeneration needed to achieve the cooperation sustainable work will require.

Day 179

We learn to show respect and deference to a greater mind than our own. We give God and nature the benefit of the doubt. We acknowledging there is no rival to God. There is no individual or group that deserves the ultimate admiration and trust that is due to the Creator of the universe alone.

Without unrivaled admiration and deference, it is not possible to approach and know God as God.

Consequently, we do not blindly trust and act upon information that comes from any source that claims to rival or replace God when solving problems and making decisions, especially about issues that concern the future. Rather, we stay open to something higher, making us available to God and God's unforeseen and wonderful purposes on earth.

Day 180

Our primary cooperative relationship must be with our Creator. It is the one we can't lose and for which there is no substitute if lost. We spare no time or effort getting this primary relationship right, just as plants spare no time or effort constantly orienting themselves to the sun. We start every day quietly enveloped in closeness to God.

It is in the experience of direct intimacy with God that we learn best about true altruism – when the giver gets no benefit, while the receiver continues to benefit. The energy from the sun is free. Plants don't have to pay for it. They grow and thrive, yet the sun gets nothing back in return. Life starts with consistent flows of unearned altruism.

Experiencing God's pure altruism firsthand, in real practical situations, sets God apart from everything and everyone else, which firmly gives God an unrivaled place in our hearts and minds. We know we owe our existence to God's but feel no burden of debt. Rather we feel gratitude and the desire to participate joyfully in the wonder of creation like we see other creatures doing. Life is funded by joy, not guilt. Life flourishes by interacting, not by controlling.

Day 181

Just as completely blocking the sun will kill a plant, blocking our connection to God, by creating rivals to God for our attention and trust, stops all growth along the cooperative pathways of life. When humans cut themselves off from their divine source, they don't stop growing. Rather their growth heads off toward a painful death.

Rivals to God form an untreated cancer in our souls.

Untreated cancer grows constantly, never pausing, but at the expense of the host.

Untreated cancer stops growing and dies only when it kills its host.

There are religions, philosophies, political and economic systems that will only die out once they have finally driven all but a few humans to extinction. The few that survive will be those who had already been cured of the cancer long before the collapse of the godless, unnatural civilization around them.

Day 182

After we have learned from nature who to admire and trust above all, we can take the next step on the pathway of life because from there we can hear something new, or at least we can hear more clearly than we did before. God's callings continue. We continue to hear and heed these callings.

God calls out to us through our sense of empathy.

We start to see the pain another life is going through and want to do something about it. Since are starting to take on the character of God, we also want to see other lives around us joyful and thriving. We feel pain when we see other lives suffering the slow loss of their God-given fulness of life. We know God better now because have moved closer to God's heart. The pain we feel is God's pain. Love feels the pain of the one loved.

Moved by empathy, we take the next step on the path of life. From there we will hear more.

Day 183

God calls out to us through our conscience. We feel pain inside when we even contemplate solving a problem by harming or neglecting another life. We sense we would not want someone to do that to us.

Moved by conscience, we take the next step. We also would not want our loved ones to be mistreated in this way, whether related to us or not. Our sense of concern expands beyond our own immediate comfort and pleasure, and beyond our own immediate circle of relationships. We start to include the well-being of an ever-larger circle of lives in how we define our own well-being.

In contrast, the godless narrow their concern down to the well-being of their own circle and then narrow it even further. Eventually there is room in their hearts for only one, whom they call "number one." When push comes to shove, they look out for number one and no one else.

The godless become their own god - a very cruel god indeed.

Day 184

When we are informed by empathy and have a functioning conscience, we don't want our loved ones to live in a society where it is normal to mistreat each other any more than we would want to live there ourselves.

The next step on the path of life is to make sure our loved ones are not harmed, and have the resources needed to grow. This includes the plants and animals that share a space with us.

Following God's example, we act out of altruism toward others, knowing that for some time, we may well receive nothing back in return. We are fine with that.

Day 185

Because we include the well-being of the lives we love in our definition of our own well-being, when they hurt we hurt. When they rejoice, we rejoice. Regardless of whether they are fully capable adults or growing children, we don't take responsibility away from them because we wouldn't want someone to do that to us. We are still responsible *to* them, but we are not responsible *for* them. They must take responsibility for their own choices. This is how they will come to meet God, through a healthy fear of doing harm by making bad choices.

However, all humans go through times when they truly cannot meet all their own needs. We are all legitimately dependent on others when we are very young, very old, sick, or injured.

When someone we care about is in one of these dependent phases we take more responsibility for their well-being when we are the ones best suited to do so, but as always in nature – we do just enough, just in time, without dely. No more, no less. Without complaint. Without drawing any attention to our actions.

Day 186

As we learn the way God treats us and how to relate to God, we find those we care about are no longer out of sight, out of mind. They are always part of us, always with us.

As we grow into a greater Godlikeness, we find ourselves naturally starting our sentences with "we" more often than "I." This is because we now define ourselves individually more by who we feel connected to, partnered with, protected by and responsible for than by what we possess, want and plan to get for ourselves in the future.

Feeling connected is key. The body protects what it can still feel and poorly protects what it can no longer feel. Societies work the same way. Humans poorly protect those lives with whom they feel no living connection, whether it be other humans or other species.

Day 187

With our kin we learn how to start with a relationship of altruism and then build a relationship of mutual benefit. Our kin benefits from our actions and eventually we benefit from theirs. Altruism does not mean coddling. We don't do things for them which they can and must do for themselves, because this sends the message that they are incapable and fragile when they are not.

Someday we won't be there, and they need to be both competent and confident enough to handle whatever situation they face. We learn not to completely protect our kin from the natural consequences of their own actions that are contrary to God's way of doing things. We don't make excuses for the harmful behavior of anyone we are related to whether they are older than us, younger than us or the same age as us.

Day 188

We don't abandon our kin when they make the same kinds of ethical mistakes we once made, often when imitating someone we admired whose selfishness seemed to pay off in the short term.

We don't say "I told you so." They already know that.

Instead, we remain available and engaged. We help them to learn the natural consequences of selfish vs. cooperative choices – when their action benefits them but provides no benefit to the other person they are relating to or even harms them. Sometimes we must be the ones to impose the consequence by limiting or ending their access to our help. For the most part we let the natural cause-and-effect dynamic set up by God do the teaching.

Selfishness always ends in pain.

We listen and provide empathy while the situation does the teaching.

Day 189

Our way of managing ethical corrections helps our kin learn to anticipate the natural consequences of spiteful choices – when a potential action will hurt both themselves and someone else.

In this way we cultivate our kin into a lifelong friend, someone we ourselves will enjoy having in our lives. By doing this we expand the network of cooperative, helpful relationships we and others, including strangers, can someday draw upon if needed.

In our kin relationships, we increase the stock of happiness everyone can count on by shutting down sources of unhappiness in the world before they get a foothold. Without any preachiness, guests notice there is something peacefully different about our family.

Day 190

As a social species God designed us to mirror the characteristics of those around us. We all do better when we all do better. We all behave better when we all behave better. Neighbors and neighborhoods exist in nature anywhere different lives and different kinds of life live alongside each other, sharing a space and its resources. Neighborly behaviors are built into our brains. We are naturally kinder and more generous in a kinder and generous neighborhood. Conversely, we are naturally meaner and stingier in a mean and stingy neighborhood. Knowing this about ourselves, we are vigilant to make our real and metaphorical neighborhoods kinder, safer and more enriching for everyone.

Taking these steps along the neighbor pathway of life draws us closer to God's heart. We enter deeper into God's natural habitat daily as we build that creative openness within our souls and between each other. God's natural habitat is a place of stable, growing, and widely shared well-being.

Living in God's natural habitat, we hear more than we ever imagined possible. And what we hear in this enriched space changes us and the direction of our lives.

Day 191

Those who have responded to all the previous callings from God are drawn close enough to hear a whisper. It seems to be carried on a fragrant breeze from beyond the horizon, beyond what we can currently see, prove, or improve. It comes from God's future, the particulars of which only God knows.

In the whisper we may even hear a life-calling. In addition to hearing and responding to God's message about why all humans exist in general, we may gain a sense of why we exist individually. We may hear a hint, and feel a general directional nudge towards the yet unrefined answer to the question we may have asked over the years in quiet, rested, honest moments...

"Why am I here?"

Day 192

Through all the other steps we have taken on the life path God has given so far, we will have observed things that trouble us in society and things that inspire us in nature. We realize we live on a beautiful planet and in an often-hideous human world. We feel stretched between what could be and what shouldn't be. This tension puts us in a unique position, one rich in original creative possibilities.

As we find ourselves placed by fate right between what currently exists and what could exist under God's direction we often feel anger and frustration. Frustration can be fruitful. Creative tension is what makes us function like the string on a guitar, when drawn tight and tuned.

In this tensed and tuned state, we stand ready and available to receive a perfectly timed touch. To our surprise and delight, at just the right moment, we gently, easily, and naturally produce the note we alone were born to play in the great symphony of life.

Day 193

If we have been willing to listen to things that are not easy to hear, to take in the pain others feel...

If we have been willing to feel small and somewhat incompetent compared to the majestic genius we see operating in healthy natural systems...

If we have been willing to see reality as it is and ourselves as we are – not useless, but not omnipotent, not ignorant, but not all-knowing.....

Then we may find ourselves right in the middle between the past and the future. This is right where God needs us to be if the future is ever to be different than the past. Our work, given, guided, and graced by God, can break the time barrier and become a vital part of a very different and better future on earth.

Day 194

We are not God, nor are we fused with God to form one entity, and we never will be. But neither are we mindless machines, built to simply produce, consume, and make the rich richer and the famous more adored.

Instead, as humans we are uniquely suited to serve as receptive, responsive instruments in the endlessly creative hands of God. We live directly adjacent to God in a state of receptive readiness. We live in a state of "at-oneness" and anticipation.

Any great musician naturally prefers a sensitive, responsive instrument to one that is not. And an instrument the musician is intimately familiar with, one that has already adjusted to the unique way the musician plays. For composers, having such an instrument ready at hand frees a musical genius to create something of sublime and original beauty.

Day 195

The farther along we are in the discipline of responsive listening, the more special are the messages we can hear and understand. Those who know we love and accept them will share secrets they share with no one else. It is no different with God.

By listening and responding quickly, competently, and ethically so far, we don't guarantee we will hear such messages, but we have increased the odds considerably. It does in fact happen. It has happened in human history.

There was always a favorite instrument at hand in the room when Mozart felt the impulse to create something amazing the world had never heard before.

It happens in natural history. In nature, the more uncommon, the more improbable and rarer an event, the more impact it has when it occurs.

Just because something is uncommon does not make it unreal or of no value.

Day 196

Deep listening and effective response are two sides of the same coin, as one naturally increases the capacity of the other.

The better we listen, the better we respond, the better we respond, the better positioned we are to hear what comes next. A life calling, if it ever comes, is a result of many, many rounds in a behavioral feedback loop. We constantly learn, from the responses we see in others, something important about the way we last behaved toward them and adjust our next behavior accordingly.

In God's way of doing things, it is common and expected for us to respond first, for years, to the general calling to ethical behavior addressed to all of humanity. It is the natural function of all humans wherever we have been placed, to care for the lives with whom we share time and space on earth.

Day 197

In any healthy organization the most advanced, interesting, and challenging assignments are reserved for those who have a long track record of doing all the basic work everyone must do reliably, thoroughly, on time with a good attitude. Those who demonstrate an ethic of high productivity and self-management, those who are low maintenance, are the ones trusted with the most significant work.

These are the ones selected to do things God is doing on earth that history alone will show to have been the most significant. It won't be apparent at the time, so the one God selects must be low maintenance. To be low maintenance means to have demonstrated the ability to manage one's own time, energy, moods, motivation, and relationships for as long as it takes to get the job done and do it well.

If anyone ever receives a more specific life calling, that person will be one who is already long accustomed to responding faithfully to the general calling given to all humans through nature, history, and empathy. It will be someone who has a solid reputation of being ethical and competent in all they do as a reflection of the excellence of God.

Day 198

God is everywhere in everything, which means God is right where we are right now. We don't need to run off to special places or events to seek our calling, especially if we are currently neglecting the basic calling God gives all of us.

We don't need to seek an audience with a guru or celebrity intellectual. Vanity works that way, but God does not. Those who receive a specific life calling will always be those who are already, constantly available, and useful to God and helpful to life right where they are.

Day 199

Specific life callings come only to those who are already doing work that garners no attention, no praise, no applause and little if any material reward. They do what they do because it needs to be done if God is to be honored on earth, not because they expect to profit from doing it.

God selects these individuals for more unique missions for a simple reason. Someone who works in anticipation of attention, admiration and material compensation will slow down or stop working if those external rewards are in doubt or stop, because that was the goal all along.

Someone who works because the work honors God and needs to be done, will keep working with or without the promise of personal reward. As always, God's happiness catches up with us later. To our surprise we find a lasting sense of meaning and contentment in our daily responsibilities. From deep inside there springs up an awareness that we have finally become someone God can trust to participate effectively in the miracle of creation.

Day 200

The worker God taps for special assignments is someone already doing something that does not give one bragging rights. It will be a totally unsuitable activity to put on public display. It will be useless as a demonstration of one's attractiveness, cleverness, or righteous superiority. It won't make good advertising copy or imagery.

God meets in secret those who labor in obscurity and calls them to something others won't easily understand or support, but something which God will support, protect, and never abandon.

It is only intrinsically valuable work, done for God's purposes, done to God's standards of excellence, done within God's ethical limits, which will earn God's sustaining involvement.

Day 201

Responding to our general calling draws us close to God's heart. There, alone in solitude we feel God's grief about what has happened to the earth. We sense God's longing for all that could have happened instead but was never given the chance to take root.

What God started was strangled in the crib, murdered by a selfish, insatiable human civilization. We see the tragedy of it all. As a bandage draws off fluids from a wound, we draw off some of the suffering of our grieving Creator. Our loving compassion brings comfort to God, the One we love more than any other or any object. Love naturally wants to enter into the suffering of the one who is loved, to soothe the pain by sharing it.

Selfishness refuses to enter into and share the suffering of another. God will not call a selfish person into service. Regardless of what esteemed institution they may work for, no matter what they claim to the contrary, selfish people are not serving God's purposes, they are serving themselves.

Day 202

Without grief and longing there is no life calling from God. Our grief is caused by the loss of something good that was once there. Our grieved longing comes from the absence of something good that has never been there, because now life on earth is stunted without it.

With a specific life calling from God, we sense there is something wrong in the world, and that we were born and equipped by our unique history to do something about it, that has not yet been done, in the way only we can. Eventually we come to see that all our previous choices and experiences were necessary to fit us to our life calling.

Day 203

The original meaning of the word "chaos" was not disorder. Rather, it meant a yawning gap, a void, a sense that something is missing. A specific life calling will be about filling a gap between what is and what could and should be.

We may sense that what we see happening in the world does not go on between creatures in healthy natural systems. Clearly it should not go on among humans, or between humans and other species. Our calling may be to replace that pattern of behavior, and the values that motivate it, with behaviors and values that are true to life.

Or we may sense something good that goes on in healthy natural systems is missing among humans. Our life calling may be to figure out how that natural process could be translated into human behaviors or systems.

Day 204

As God's life-calling for us awakens within us, we may sense the current human understanding of something in nature or history is flawed in some way. We may feel an urgency to correct and update human understanding with new, accurate information so humanity can again access the genius of God imbedded in nature and history, thus proving accurate models to guide our priorities.

Whatever form it takes, a calling from God will always be creative in some way. God is *The Creator*, after all. God's core activity is being creative, constantly creating. A calling will not involve copying, extending, preserving, or updating old, out-lived solutions - solutions that have caused more problems than they solved.

To be close to God is to be close to a creative work. Divinely given and guided work always culminates in something timely, useful, and original in at least one important way.

Day 205

Following our calling, we come to see that what makes us different is the same thing that can make a difference over time. Our divergence from what everyone else is and does is no flaw or failure. It is our gift.

What makes us different is what allows us to contribute something different from what was done in the past. We don't owe God anything for this gift. Debt and repayment exists only between equals. We are not God's equal. God lacks nothing. What could we ever give back that God needs? Plants don't owe the sun anything or try to give anything back to the sun.

Instead, plants use a capacity only plants have and imitate the sun's overwhelming generosity in their own unique, irreplaceable way. Just as the sun gives plants what they can't give themselves, plants, by turning sunlight into sugars and oxygen, give all other lives on earth what they can't give themselves.

We do the same thing. We use our unique combination of abilities and experiences to provide for other lives what no other life they know will be able to do. What makes our work unique is how it fits the needs of the present situation. Fitting the need of the situation often requires us to enter into a scene touched by tragedy.

Day 206

If our natural empathetic insight is regenerating through daily contact with God and nature, tragedy will call out to us. We find we can't *not* care about what is happening. We find we are incapable of being indifferent, even as those around us shrug and easily find a way to overlook it or go along with it all. Many even profit from it and are very proud of that fact.

The deep, irresistible, empathetic pull of tragedy helps explain our own existence and the uniqueness of our journey to date. We know firsthand the cruel, unjust, damaging touch of godlessness. We feel the pain other victims are feeling because we have felt it ourselves and still live with its bitter scars as memorials to the rule of selfishness on earth.

Tragedy is the word that describes what goes on before the godly have made their new contribution to building a broad-based justice. Tragedy is what happens before the godly have replaced something unnatural that doesn't work with something natural that does. Tragedy is the chaotic gap between a lovely planet and a loveless society. We find ourselves drawn into that gap.

Day 207

What is going on is tragic because it was never inevitable or necessary. Things could have been different if different choices had been made, if there had been better options to choose from. If there had been living human models courageous enough to make better choices.

In response to the pull of tragedy we think..

"Somebody needs to do something. Now. Here. Something new. Something different than what everyone else is doing. It doesn't matter if anyone notices or follows. It doesn't matter if it doesn't pay anything. It doesn't matter how big it is. What matters is that there is someone doing something different in spite of all the reasons to do nothing or go along with what is happening. By God's grace, I will use what I have, where I am placed, to do something that at least relieves some of the suffering. And if I can, I will be part of creating something that puts an end to this tragedy and replaces it with something just and beautiful. I can't do anything else and live with myself. God help me."

Day 208

We keep doing what we can do about the tragedy even though nothing gets much better, at least not for a long time.

But precisely because we are not just complaining about things, but actually doing something, however small and unnoticed, a better behavioral option exists somewhere on earth, at least in seed form.

Tragedy continues and grows worse during the long timespan before the better option is finally accepted and used as the normal way to do things. This broad acceptance usually happens long after the originator dies. The one who brings the new idea dies but the new idea does not.

Day 209

It is almost impossible to kill a really good idea, one that accurately reflects reality and draws its inspiration from the wisdom embodied in nature. A truly good idea is true to life, and it works when implemented. Bad ideas are not true, so they don't bear logical scrutiny and require that people turn off their brains and accept nonsense to "follow God." Bad ideas also don't work when implemented. Bad ideas never actually deliver what they promise. Bad ideas won't bear the weight of responsibility for the well-being of other lives.

Bringing a better idea starts with protest and moves to experimentation. We are honest and say, at least to ourselves,

"What this society is doing is false. It is based on lies. What society is doing doesn't work. It creates more problems than it solves. It is the root cause of the tragedy we see. We choose to abandon those ideas and try something else. This is what we think is truer to reality and we want to try it out to see if it works better."

We are accused of heresy. We are called rebels. But God does not accuse us. God calls us and helps us at critical moments, demonstrating what work is and is not authorized by the true ultimate authority.

Day 210

A truly better idea can effectively guide behavior within a constantly changing situation. It does not require conditions that haven't existed for centuries to be relevant and to work. A really good idea must emerge from protest and reform.

Daring souls will take up the challenge to try out the idea and make it work even better. Taking this social risk makes more sense when one is young and has yet to build a life based on the old system, so there is less to lose. If it works, there is a whole life to be gained that will be better than it could have been under the old system.

In history many moral innovators were young, but all of them are young at heart. Those that are older have seen fads come and go, promises made and broken. For them, even though they have more to lose they do it anyway for God's sake and for the sake of the young.

Once the new idea has been proven to be true and better in the lives of a few moral pioneers, it can live on in memory, nourished by passion, stored in the obscure but true stories about godly and noble lives.

Day 211

We may be forced underground, we may be driven away from the fertile valleys up into the mountains, but we are still here, alive and growing stronger. So are the ideas we have proven to be from God, stored in safety, awaiting their moment.

Push an inflated ball deeper and deeper into the dark cold water and once released, it will rise even faster to the surface, break the surface and surge high into the open air, bathed in sunlight.

True, good, functional ideas gain force under the pressure of an oppressive, exploitive regime. The very actions the regime takes to suppress the new idea only proves how depraved the regime is, while making it even clearer that the new idea was better all along and cannot be killed.

Day 212

Tragedy is when the vast majority wake up each day to misery and deprivation, fighting to just survive, unable to even think about the future, much less work on it.

Tragedy happens under the rule of money and the insatiable drive for more money. Under the rule of money only the privileged few enjoy a pleasant and safe present reality. They have the luxury of worrying about the future and claiming to work on it productively.

Under God's rule everyone has what they need to survive and grow into what God guides them to be. They wake up each day refreshed, to a life containing enough safety and enough possibility that they have a reason to live. When called upon to do so, under God's rule, everyone is equipped to work on the future productively.

Day 213

The rule of money always creates broad based exploitation that takes many forms, up to and including actual slavery. A civilization built on any kind of exploitation is unsustainable.

Apart from God, all sustainability work will turn out to be unsustainable.

Future-focused work, designed and managed without any thought of a daily, responsive listening relationship with God, is a personal vanity project at best, and participation in a coercive, utopian cult at worst.

God alone knows the future. It hasn't formed yet so it isn't possible for us to know the future, much less how to create a better one. There are just so many variables that can affect the outcome that only an unlimited mind can account for them all and guide our daily efforts. In time, small local actions can have enormous effects globally.

It doesn't matter how high or low we are in the current social hierarchy. If we are higher up and work disconnected from God, we will simply make larger mistakes, impacting more people in more places, for longer, whether we intended to or not.

Day 214

To our surprise, even with a better idea in hand, we find callings from God do not focus our attention and efforts primarily toward an envisioned future.

We find instead we are primarily focused on our actions in the present. We are not given the future to manage or create. The master plan is held in the mind of God, not in ours. Afterall, we may not live past today and the plan must be held somewhere that isn't going away.

Today is all we are given for sure. God calls us today to embody the wisdom and justice of God today, each time we interact with any life or manage any resource necessary for life.

We are called to make the most of anything useful we are entrusted with, while reducing waste as much as possible. In nature nothing is wasted. Everything essential for life is recycled over and over.

Day 215

We live daily as called and guided creatures. For the most part we live out the general calling that applies to all humans. In addition to, not in place of our general calling, some of our activities may enact a specific calling once it has come into our lives.

Living as called creatures daily, we discover an unforeseen and unplanned future begins to emerge before our eyes. It is different from what would have occurred if we followed our own notions or those of the culture around us. Smaller and hidden, it is still more interesting and better than anything we could possibly have foreseen or planned. We grow daily in our admiration of the Unseen Designer.

Day 216

Under God's rule, sustainability work is not about the future. It is about right here, right now, embedded in the unique way we treat each other under all circumstances. A true and good idea is one that we can fully implement right now, right where we are.

In nature, life introduces new forms of itself in one place, at one time, using local resources to deal with the immediate and emerging situation. Following life's lead, we know that if an idea cannot be implemented until everyone is forced to use it by the government, or bribed to use it by the market, it is not from God, not natural, not true, and not good.

If right here, today, through our ethical and practical actions, our situation becomes even slightly less destructive and more cooperative, then we are setting in motion a different future than would have developed had we not been involved.

This is the way futures change in nature.

Day 217

There is a pathway to harm and pathway to health. Ideas spread as they are handed off between contemporaries and handed on to the next generation. This pattern holds whether the ideas are true and good or false and bad.

Since misery loves company, damaged people damage people so they have others around they can relate to. Abandoned people abandon people in their time of need because they think that is what one does when love costs something. Sickened and hurt people sicken and hurt people so their pain in common to complain about. Deceived people deceive people so there is no one around to point the way out of a system of illusions and lies. Dominated people dominate people as soon as they get the chance because they always envied the power of their oppressors. Excluded people exclude people to experience the pleasure they assume those who excluded them from something get to feel. Exploited people exploit people because they saw how easy life was for those who stole their labor from them and want that ease for themselves.

Day 218

Apart from direct contact with God humans lack the power to break free from cycles of selfishness and hate.

Those separated from God create closed-off structures that separate people from God. Those made less human by inhuman systems from the past create dehumanizing systems to control the future. It is natural to hate such behaviors, but we remember that we once did the same things and were powerless to stop ourselves for long. Our victimizers are victims themselves.

The difference is with us, somehow God used pain to break through the denial we used to not see how damaged we were and how much we lacked. The absence of full humanness is excruciating. Our victimizers are in pain. If we were not beyond the reach of God's mercy, neither are they. The most damaged, hardened land can spring back to life if you can get water to it.

We may need to put distance between ourselves and those who would harm our lives, but we must stand ready to open our hearts to them should God open their hearts to what is true and good.

Day 219

Helped people help people. People enfolded in God's care enfold people in their care. Healed people heal people. Guided people guide people reliably to good places and enriching, free experiences. Empowered people empower people. Wanted and included people include people and make them feel wanted and valued for who they are. Liberated and fulfilled people liberate people and help them find their way to their own unique fulfillment.

Those connected to God and nature help create simple open-ended social experiences that invite people to connect directly to God, with little if any planning or stagecraft.

Those becoming fully human again through daily contact with God, inspired by nature, create humanizing, evolving, social ecosystems designed to create and share a future that gets increasingly better for everyone and everything.

Day 220

There are days when we don't feel available to or interested in any higher calling because we feel so low, so overwhelmed, and defeated. Yet because we have been responding to God's callings, we sense we are welcome to approach and call out to God in all our confusion and pain.

We have learned God answers and can penetrate any storm of madness we may feel.

Some of the worst prisons are the prisons we create in our own minds.

God can return us to a productive sanity no matter how strongly confusion and pain seem to envelope us. God sets prisoners free, but in a particular way. God shows us where, when, and how to dig our way out, then meets us halfway from the other side. We don't wait passively to be liberated from any prison we find ourselves in, but neither do we make it all the way out without help. Historically, generations that inherit freedom without effort let it go with an indifferent shrug if a movement comes along that promises easy comfort, entertainment, and heaps of stuff in exchange for their God-given rights.

In contrast, historically the newly freed, who actively struggled to achieve freedom, know the value of freedom in a way that those who inherited freedom can't. The newly freed refuse to ever lose freedom again without a fight.

Day 221

As long as we continue to seek, receive, and respond to God's callings, we find God hears and responds to us when we call out.

Usually not instantly, because we are not yet ready to fully appreciate and attend to what we will hear.

We find a quiet place. We remove all rival voices and messages. We stop, wait, and listen. It is like listening for a whisper coming from somewhere behind a thin sheet of fabric.

At the right time, not too far in advance, not too late to act, we hear something amazingly relevant and useful. It is not a general suggestion. It is precise and particular to our situation at the moment. Because it is so perfectly fitted to our situation, we feel ourselves met, touched, taught, and helped by God. Intimate help is help that is precisely timed and very particular.

In a way that can't be predicted, bottled, or mass-produced, God intimately helps those who intimately help others in their lives, always showing up at the right time and place to do what needs to be done the way it needs to be done.

Day 222

When we cry out to God, we learn that God's help does not cost money. God's help is not just another privilege of the already privileged, excluding those without discretionary income.

God's help is simple, but it is always just enough, just in time; perfectly fitted to the unique situation we face today.

God's help always involves doing what we can do today, using our current abilities and resources. If not today, then in the very near future. We won't have to wait long to do the next helpful thing.

Day 223

Some of us are slow learners! It takes several rounds before we realize that every time we stop seeking and responding to God's direction, because it means changing how we behave in some way, God goes completely silent. Now, when we pray, it is like listening to hear a whisper coming from somewhere behind a 10-foot wall of concrete. Either we hear nothing at all, or we hear nothing useful and relevant. We feel abandoned.

Isolated and cut off, we are on our own, engulfed in all our limitations and worst fears.

God does not help those who have no intention of helping God, showing up only to help themselves. God opposes those who intend to harm other lives to get what they want.

Day 224

When we cut ourselves off from God's intimate, ethical guidance, we become easy prey to cunning humans who offer guidance and help. In return they require either money, adulation, attention, or labor. Often they demand some escalating combination of all our resources. They demand lifetime loyalty, even when it requires overlooking and excusing their deceitful and harmful behaviors. We become enablers, complicit in their crimes through our silence and often through our actions.

Disloyalty to God sets us up to be commandeered by other people to serve their interests, not ours. They have no interest in releasing us to serve our calling and won't let us go without an ugly struggle. It's better to break off and go back to where we left off, changing our behaviors until we have created a mutually beneficial relationship with those God has already placed in our lives, even it requires pure altruism for a while.

God meets us every step of the way back to the path of life and in the process turns our once wandering hearts into deeply loyal hearts.

Day 225

Periodically, as we go farther on our journey of sustainability we need to stop and re-pack our bags. We need to unload some things we won't need and replace them with things we will need at every turn.

All the relational pathways life will take will be built on voluntary, ongoing, satisfying reciprocity. None will be harmful or exploitive. All healthy, productive relationships are mutually beneficial.

Mutually beneficial relationships are built and maintained through cycles of mutual influence.

From the response of others, we learn how to be even more precisely helpful and cooperative.

We will learn progressively more about how to learn with and from others. We will get better and better at making timely use of the feedback we get from others in response to our own actions.

Day 226

In a healthy relationship each party's responses help influence, adjust and improve the way the other party behaves when solving problems, both practical and social.

In a true partnership, each of us unlearn old patterns of behaviors, replacing them with new and better ones. Together we honestly evaluate how well our existing ways of doing things work to meet the challenges of our situation and make adjustments as needed.

Although we are honest, we are still careful with our words. Although we are polite, we are still honest about what isn't working.

We are called to be both factually honest and socially constructive and we work to live up to this standard when dealing with any and every challenge we face together.

Day 227

There is a built-in corrective in a healthy partnership. If the way we do things does not meet both our needs now, or won't do so soon, we don't consider it a workable solution. We stop the work on the problem we are trying to solve and go to work on our working relationship. We make changes in what we have been doing until the way we treat each other works for us both equally. This is only fitting because we are equal members of a team.

Once our relationship is mutually beneficial and equally influential we discover a new ability to solve problems. We can now return to the problem we were solving and move through it productively by fashioning original and better solutions.

When we are connected to God, see ourselves as part of nature, and treat each other well, we are able to create a sustainable future we can share together, one that is not static, but one that is constantly renewing itself by taking on new forms.

Day 228

God made us a social species for a reason. God gave us brains, observational powers, and a sense of empathy for a reason. We were made to learn from, engage in, and adjust to a range of situations beyond what any other species is capable of. Only by doing this meaningful and essential work do we discover how our lives contribute to a sustainable future for all forms of life on earth.

There are no magical or religious short cuts to a more promising future on earth. If we are still in the habit of ignoring God's direction to stop behaviors that harm other lives, we will not know the guiding presence of God. If God were to draw close and answer requests while we are still in such a state of moral decay that would only encourage us to keep behaving in destructive ways. God never gives the green light to, ever overlooks evil.

God is not our personal assistant. God is not our group's sponsor. God does not exist to expedite our own personal well-being or to secure the well-being of our group at the expense of all others.

We abandon all dead-end paths and get on with the daily work of re-learning to do what we were originally created to do. We choose to do nothing less and nothing else and find to our surprise that everything alive around us gets happier and healthier. This in turn makes us happier and healthier.

Day 229

We accept that every natural life path we will take from here will require skill and work to build the kind of mutual benefit and mutual influence relationships that lead to constant growth and change.

If we take on this way of life all at once, we are overwhelmed. It is exhausting even to think about.

But if we take on this way of life in 24-hour increments, we find we are refreshed and refueled enough to live this way for another day. There are unforeseen moments of rest, renewal, and delight. These moments are set aside for us, unforeseen by us. These moments fill us with relief and gratitude and sometimes thrill us with surprise.

It is enough. Under God's rule what is enough is the same as what will survive. What will survive will go on to replace what can't survive. What can't survive will inevitably collapse under the weight of its own injustice.

Day 230

We continue to re-pack our bags before continuing our journey on God's life pathways. Another item we must remove if we are to go any further toward sustainability is any false notion of how God views differences between creatures.

God is the Creator and as such, is invested equally in the well-being of all creation, all creatures. Any notion that God plays favorites and supports dominating hierarchies on earth is a lie created by criminals. Promoting such a cruel lie is slander, a crime against God that always results in crimes against some part of creation.

God does not commune with criminals or dwell in the midst of a society bent on criminal ends. God does not dwell among a society that revels in its ability to use criminal methods to get rich by harming the innocent. God has nothing to do with cunning lies and oppressive violence.

Day 231

There is no ceremony or ritual that can change God's mind about injustice and make God complicit in vast crimes organized and endorsed by a society. It makes no difference if the entity endorsing criminal acts is an old religion. It makes no difference whether the entity organizing criminal acts is the market or the state.

Criminal societies are always built on some form of idolatry – worshiping a man-made god. False gods are usually gods of fertility/prosperity. Worshiping fertility/prosperity does not require any concern for justice. It just requires lust – wanting more of everything forever. God is not a god of fertility. God is the God of Justice. Justice brings about thriving diversity. Thriving diversity sustains fertility.

Going straight for more fertility/prosperity has never produced more justice, later. Rather, it tramples justice underfoot.

Justice brings about enough fertility over time because justice creates high diversity combined with a high level of mutually beneficial relationships between different forms of life. Justice also simultaneously retains each life form's own protected space and resources.

Justice is what allows each form and community of life to become what it is, to do what it does and to eventually become what it will become next.

Day 232

In God's economy, justice produces just enough fertility and prosperity to keep us growing, but not so much that moral growth becomes unnecessary, and not so little prosperity that moral growth becomes impossible.

The human soul slackens, degenerates, and becomes destructive whenever and wherever there is too much prosperity. Soaked in money and intoxicated by the illusion of unlimited power, we lose our sense of healthy dependence on a mind greater than our own, on each other, and on an environment we didn't create and can't replace if lost.

Day 233

Soaked in money and luxury, we come to believe we know better than God. We try to use our wealth to force the environment to adjust to us, making our own lives easier and more comfortable, while making the lives of others unsustainable. Any natural God-given ability that we turn off and stop using, we quickly lose – forever.

The rich-in-money tend to observe and admire each other, so they often lose the ability to observe and admire nature. Consequently, they are far less likely to imitate its efficient genius.

Historically, the rich-in-money didn't need or use empathy, so they quickly lost it. They don't need to demonstrate cooperation; they can use bribes and threats to get what they want. By the third generation there is often no empathy or cooperation left in most families rich-in-money, except for show. Instead, they care most about their standing among other people rich-in-money, so real social virtues are replaced with calculated indifference, and cunning cruelty. All this social degradation flows from a lie about what constitutes being rich.

In contrast, God teaches us the truth about natural richness. We learn to be ever richer in wisdom, in kindness, in cooperative skill, in constructive creativity. God is rich in all these ways, and we learn to be more and more like God.

Day 234

When humans have too much prosperity, they come to believe life is only about producing and consuming more. The goal becomes to have a big enough pile of money so that someday they can stop producing and just consume anything and everything they want, just the way they want it.

God help any other life that gets in the way of someone bent on building a big enough pile of money so they and their young can do nothing but consume for the rest of their lives.

We neither admire nor aspire to imitate those who have "achieved" a life of total consumption, any more than we would admire a cancerous tumor. The word for cancer was once "consumption," for good reason. Human empathy and with it the ability to cooperate with each other, are eaten away from the inside out when we make our individual lives and our collective societies about nothing but consuming more and more.

Day 235

Since we, as a regenerating humanity, live in constant contact with God and nature, we experience constant rediscovery of what God designed humans to do, naturally, as part of earth.

It becomes natural for us to oppose the rich-in-money with God's demand for justice, defined as doing what it takes to protect the natural diversity life requires to sustain itself and grow.

Historically, the rich-in-money have tried to exploit the poor and/or the natural environment a little more every year to become even richer. The poor and the environment are the mine the rich-in-money plan to exploit to get even richer. Taking a little more over time, by force, from a vast number of powerless people, while giving nothing back, has always been the path to great, multigenerational fortunes. The other path has been exploiting more of the natural environment, while doing nothing to restore it to health afterwards.

Eventually both sources of wealth are tapped out and retaliate in some way.

To be governed by the rich-in-money is the road to ruin. We do not worship the rich-in-money. They are not God.

Day 236

It is only when a society prioritizes God's demand for justice over its own desire for prosperity that it has a solid place to stand. We stand on God's law and stand up against the rich to prevent them from harming the poor. We don't stand alone. God is with us and nature itself is our ally in the struggle.

Aside from God's divine charter for humanity, there is no other basis of authority strong enough, nor place to stand that will not give way under the pressure of anxiety and envy.

A society that severs its connection to God as the ultimate authority finds it has no authority that will hold in its hour of crisis, because all efforts apart from God eventually succumb to the rule of the rich-in-money.

Every man has his price whose soul does not rest fully on God's faithfulness.

Day 237

As an emerging new humanity, we must take a different path. The path of life. We take our stand firmly on God's demand for justice. We trust God's promise to dwell among and reward any group, of any size, anywhere, at any time, who pursue justice first.

We seek enough prosperity. No more, no less. Our goal is to participate in the continuous forward motion of life on life's terms.

We do not seek more than life requires to keep moving itself forward in its own amazing and creative way. There is a natural, shared happiness that comes with natural sufficiency.

Neither will we support harming or removing what life requires to keep moving forward, in all its forms. There is unnatural lonely suffering that comes with unnatural deprivation.

Day 238

We match the leap in human brain power that happened some time back in human evolution with a leap in moral power that is happening in and among us right now. Better late than never!

The moral force awakening in us is a strong, natural drive that is showing up exactly when it is supposed to. It may seem somewhat late on the scene, but it has arrived just in time.

This new moral force is as natural and essential for survival as the sex drive. Children naturally enter puberty and are surprised and confused to suddenly feel the full force of sexual desire.

As part of the same natural process at the species level, we feel ourselves passing from a state of latent moral force that used empty words into a state of strong and active moral force. We find we can now make firm decisions and build habits that expand our options to grow both the diversity and the complex integration of life.

Our job in the garden is not to find and eat the biggest juiciest piece of fruit before anyone else gets to it. Our job is to make sure there will be many kinds of fruit, for many generations, everywhere we take up residence.

Day 239

If having too much prosperity causes trouble, so does having too little. The human soul degenerates whenever and wherever there is too little prosperity to go around. With too little prosperity there is no hope for a better future for oneself and one's loved ones.

Hopelessness from having too little breeds either helplessness or rage, or both. Feeling desperate and helpless can easily cause us to want a quick escape from our situation even if that means harming someone else.

Helplessness can erode our sense of dignity, our own sense of self-reliance, and the self-respect and initiative that comes from self-reliance. Those with healthy, natural, God-given dignity expect to contribute actively to their own liberation, to find their own answers, to cultivate their own resources, and to create their own solutions to their own problems.

In a regenerating state, we sense that independence and freedom are linked. We sense that if others can provide everything for us they can also withhold everything from us at any moment, unless we do what they want – which may well be in direct opposition to what God wants and what life needs.

Day 240

When we turn off our dignity we don't see what we can do today, right where we are, with what little we have, to make our situation a bit more hopeful. We neglect to build something today which we can build on later, to make our situation even more hopeful.

When we lose self-reliance we get unhealthy, unnatural dependency in return. With unhealthy, unnatural dependency comes control, and with control comes exploitation. With exploitation comes greater, unnatural weakness. With greater weakness comes more unhealthy, unnatural dependency.

Anytime we outsource a vital human function to others, we lose far more than we gain. We must not outsource our own direct first-hand experience, or our own thinking and choosing. We must not outsource our own trial-and-error learning.

We must not outsource our relationship to God, nature, and each other. Outsourcing vital human functions leaves us with impoverished minds and souls.

Poverty of mind and soul leaves us unwilling and unable to protect the natural complexity of our physical environment. Our physical environment degrades and finally collapses. Our poverty of mind and soul causes us to horde what little is left, causing widespread material poverty.

Day 241

It is only by doing our own work, by making our own mistakes and our own discoveries that we create true richness, the richness of mind and spirit that grows out of close relationships. Those who are rich-in-relationships provide a different, higher kind of leadership for those around them. Richness of mind and spirit can and will, in time, find a way to get out of material poverty and stay out, even if that means migrating to another place and starting over.

In history there have been groups that were pushed to the margins and forced to move to places where the soil was too poor to grow very much. A few of them developed new technologies, new arts and new sciences that allowed them to thrive in a totally new way. Had they not kept their dignity alive, they would have been unable to create what benefited not just themselves, but all of humanity.

Day 242

Too little prosperity can cultivate a deep hopelessness in individuals and groups, if it goes on long enough. The helplessness that comes from hopelessness can easily cause humans to prey on each other, becoming just like the rich-in-money who prey on them. Prospering by hurting others requires that we first turn off our empathy, blinding us to our own role in creating even more cynical hopelessness in our community.

Both poverty and riches can degrade the soul. With too much or too little prosperity we lose the natural God-given ability to make real, living connections with other lives. We stop forming real, mutually beneficial relationships. The degradation of poverty and riches fall the hardest on the children who grow up either in the grip of deprivation or luxury. For the children of the rich-in-money and the poor alike, unnatural, unhelpful, dysfunctional social behavior can be seen as normal – it is all they have ever seen.

Those with too much prosperity will not willingly give up their luxuries to take care of those who have too little prosperity. Those with too little prosperity cannot do much to change their situation, they are too exhausted trying to survive another day. It falls to those in the middle, with enough prosperity, but not too much, to do the hard long-term work required to create a better way to distribute resources, a system that more closely resembles how resources are distributed in nature, with no waste.

Day 243

Fertility and prosperity obsessed societies make a mockery of justice, yet they find to their horror that in time they get exactly what they deserve. Justice is still built into the very structure of existence because choices have consequences.

A society can set its priorities in opposition to God's priorities. Every society is free to choose its path, but no society is free to choose the consequences of its choices. The consequences of our actions are built-in, set-in motion by the actions themselves. This is especially true of our habitual, repetitive actions.

Day 244

Societies that give lip service to justice, but never actually achieve justice between different forms of life, are essentially just large, organized crime syndicates. Unsustainable societies are an organized gang of thugs, with a veneer of fancy elites who come up with fancy arguments to justify criminal behavior on a grand scale.

It makes no difference how pretty their buildings, how eloquent their words, or how extravagant their public performances. Force is not freedom. Thugs are not heroes.

God abandons criminals and criminal societies, leaving them to their own devices. This condemns them to oblivion. The natural consequences of their choices inevitably culminate in their own extinction.

In contrast, we, as an emerging new humanity, worship the true God, the God of justice, not a contrived god of fertility/prosperity. We take the side of God and nature at every fork in the road, in every issue that impacts the lives of others. We work to make sure all the lives around us have enough prosperity so that they can survive and grow into what the Creator designed them to be.

Day 245

For all the lives around us, human and otherwise, we work to make sure they have enough prosperity to keep growing naturally. Having enough prosperity increases the odds that someday they will experience the arrival of the new, strong moral drive God has scheduled to awaken in our species.

Those who awaken out of deprivation bring with them the keenest sense of what values must never again be allowed to take root in a society, starting with the family unit. We stop falsehood and injustice when it first shows up. We don't wait until it has grown into a massive social tumor. We stop evil where it starts – in the family system.

Day 246

God designed us so the most natural route cooperative helpfulness takes is through kin-relationships. We spare no effort to make the most of this powerful natural gift.

In a two-parent family both parents must share power equally. Neither parent is beyond being questioned or challenged by any member of the family using observation, facts, feelings, and logic. Gender makes no difference in our distribution of power. Neither does birth order or age.

Among us, no one is allowed to dominate using anger, contempt, or the threat of making everyone miserable until they get their way. There is no forced stupidity allowed among us. If the choice is not the best one given our shared situation it is not the best one no matter who wants it, or how badly they want it, or how long we have done it that way.

We confront and stop coercive behavior immediately and make it clear it will never be allowed again without consequences. Among us reason prevails, and ethics break any tie.

Day 247

In our families, siblings are equal, none receives more or less than an equal share of the family's resources. To do anything else is unjust and would imprint arbitrary, unjust, and unequal treatment as a normal way of solving problems. Our children's impressionable minds would then accept and support unjust and unequal systems in society when they become adults.

As we do the work of justice, keeping in step with God, we have learned by experience that we will be provisioned daily.

As we live as a productive part of nature, we know there will somehow be enough prosperity to go around, so we reject arrangements that make some rich by making others poor because of an accident of birth. Being first does not make someone best suited to lead. Leadership ability must still be proven through results.

Day 248

Arbitrary and fixed domination structures, where one person gets to tell another what to do without challenge just because of that person's gender or age, can lead to a kind of "stability." It appears as if conflict ends, temporarily, but it just goes underground and simmers.

Domination structures that seem to end arguments and produce peace and order lead us to believe that cooperation is not necessary, but is rather just a nice, time-consuming, frustrating option. Since it seems so much easier and faster to just force one person's desire on everyone, we stop learning and using the tools of cooperation needed to innovate. Without the tools to innovate, we stop creating new ways of living that better meet our changing situation. This prevents us from achieving the best new ways of managing our present and facing our future. Stagnation is the result.

The way God designed life to work, the best new ways of living keep open the possibility for ever better ways of living in the future. People will even start working on new ways of living early, before there is a crisis, when the cost is the lowest and the gain is the highest. All this natural innovation is lost when arbitrary, fixed domination structures govern. The specific innovation that never happened as a result is usually the very one that would have allowed the society to survive, had it been allowed to emerge.

Day 249

Just because the majority endorses something does not make it good and beyond reproach. Just because the market rewards something does not make it wise and beyond critique. Just because a celebrity does something does not make it smart or ethical to imitate.

A domination structure exists wherever it is forbidden to question how things are done or suggest there is a better way. The result is forced stupidity which always causes unnecessary harm to life.

Forced stupidity is the result whether what can't be challenged is a living male or female, an ancient or futuristic vision, popular or huge. Forced stupidity is still stupid even if it is built into everything a society does.

If I find I can't question assumptions and decisions without paying high price socially I know I am dealing with an unjust, unnatural, ungodly, unsustainable, rigid, and doomed human dominance structure. The sooner I leave the sooner I can start living closer to God, informed by the wisdom I see in natural living systems.

The longer I wait to leave, the more likely it is I will never escape and learn to live differently.

Day 250

Domination structures, starting in the family system, are a root cause of human moral degeneration. Domination structures stop the development of empathy and ethics strong enough to match human intellectual development. When intellect grows stronger than empathy, when knowledge grows faster than wisdom, the result is a civilization that relies on gimmicks, elaborate shows and shiny new technologies, not on God and healthy participation in nature.

Domination structures turn humans into no more than dead parts of a dead and lethal machine.

As soon as it becomes dangerous to suggest some person, group, institution, gender, theory or technology could be wrong, a domination structure has taken root.

God alone is omniscient and infallible. To suggest anyone else is infallible and beyond reproach is to condemn ourselves to live outside the guiding, protecting presence of God. Disaster awaits.

We refuse to participate in domination structures of any kind.

Day 251

We lose what we don't use and that includes the habits of freedom.

We can use one mode of living for so long we never use a different one. In so doing we lose the ability to choose differently. An individual or group must compete enough against rivals for resources to establish a place to live, and to fight off invasion and domination by another individual or group. For groups, his competitive effort requires cooperation. Once successful, it is time to move on to the next way of living – an even higher kind of winning.

In God's design, we move on to constructive cooperation. Once we have learned how to cooperate while remaining different, we can move on to construction. We can work together to construct an ever larger, richer, more complex habitat in which more and more forms of life can thrive and in which surprising new forms can emerge. Evolution continues to function as life designed itself to ensure its own survival. No evolution, no survival.

Artificial dominance structures stop evolution, so we oppose and remove any fixed dominance structure as soon as it shows up among us. Debt and markets are artificial dominance structures which exist nowhere in nature – for a reason.

Day 252

We do not acknowledge the right of creditors or merchants to control what we do with our God-given lives. They are not God, do not behave the way life does, and do not know what must be valued most by a species if it is to survive for long. We will find another way into the future besides borrowing, trading, and haggling.

Every other long-lived social species has found a sustainable way to move and exchange resources between each other to benefit each other. There is no reason we can't as well as long as we continue to seek and follow God's daily direction.

Day 253

There is an open, undefined space that becomes available when we remove arbitrary, unearned, and rigid dominance structures. All we are losing is a source of loss. These dead structures have never produced high diversity + high organization, the very fingerprint of God.

The new open space is a kind of chaos, pulsing with new possibilities. It is ambiguous and unfamiliar. What works there works by indirect action that produces initially invisible results that become visible results in time, not direct action that produces visible results immediately.

The Creator is the one who knows how to turn chaos into a new and higher order and has prepared us to assist in the effort. By staying close by God's side and firmly aligned with God's priorities we can tolerate the ambiguity until new and better social structures start to present themselves.

Paradoxically, we only learn how to take effective indirect action when we are in direct personal contact with a real, ambiguous situation. It is in this state alone that we feel vividly and personally the need for God's omniscient guidance. We can't learn how to participate in creation when we stay safely removed from real situations, seeing them only as abstract, academic exercises.

Day 254

Those who actually *do* things can unlearn what doesn't work and learn new ways of doing things that do work. Doers are nimble and respond quickly to an opportunity to do something new that gets better results while wasting fewer resources.

Nimbleness and sustainability go hand in hand. The nimble are those who survive and find a way to thrive after civilizations collapse under their own weight. The rigid, who never unlearn and remove anything, and the stubborn who never do anything new and different, are those who cease to exist after a collapse.

Those who never actually *do* anything can't unlearn what doesn't work. Lacking the sting of failure, they are not motivated to go find new things that work better in the real, constantly changing world.

Day 255

Once we are fully committed to life on life's terms, once we are ready to oppose any rigid, artificial mechanisms that are contrary to life's way of sustaining itself, we are ready to learn more about the first relational life path God has already put in place for us, inside us. With our heads cleared of cultural nonsense that blocks our view down the path, we can pick up speed.

For long periods of our lives, we live in daily contact with someone who shares our genetics. Besides the relationship we maintain with God and nature, a kin-relationship is the life pathway we naturally use the next most often, and these relationships last as long or longer than almost any other kind.

It is in these kin relations that it makes the most sense to put into practice what we learn from contact with God in nature. It is here that these applied insights are most likely to combine and accumulate into a healthy natural system that would compare favorably to any other natural system. It is here we will have the most frequent opportunity to experience the direct rule of God in our social world.

Day 256

It is common that in kin-relationships we first learn something about creating satisfying, mutually-beneficial relationships. It is also in kin-relationships that we first experience the inability to create satisfying relationships and the heartbreak that can bring.

A mutually-beneficial kin-relationship can be one of the most delightful relationships we ever have. And when we can't create these types of relationships with our kin we find ourselves in some of the most painful situations we ever face. If we stay in the relationship we painfully lose something we need to grow. If we leave the relationship we painfully lose something we need to be fully happy.

Any social arrangement in which every day brings a new, painful loss of something we need to be fully human is not one God designed.

We look out for this pattern of reactions in any relationship.

Surprised – hurt - angry – sad.

When we see it happen three times we know we are in trouble.

We call out to God for guidance and help.

Day 257

Pain and loss instruct us in ways that nothing else can. We don't forget the lessons we learn through pain and loss. We forget the lessons that cost us nothing in terms of personal struggle. Easy come, easy go. We fight hard to hang on to wisdom that was hard won.

There is almost nothing that teaches us more wisdom than compare-and-contrast lessons. If I see one garden that produces lots of large, beautiful vegetables and then see one the same size that doesn't produce much and what it produces is small and misshapen, that is no accident. Something is happening in the productive garden that isn't happening in the unproductive one. Something is happening in the unproductive garden that doesn't happen in the productive one. It is not random. It is being caused, especially if I notice the same pattern of different outcomes year after year despite changes in the weather over those years. Now I want to know why the differences in outcomes exist. It is a mystery.

Healthy humans can't resist a good mystery, especially one they discovered themselves through their own vivid experiences. Compare-and-contrast lessons naturally cause curious, honest humans to seek answers that are not currently available.

"Why?" questions, arising from our own direct personal experiences, often form the seed of a life-calling planted in a fertile mind. We have to find out why good things emerge and get better on some social paths while good things wither and die on other social paths, replaced by bad things that get worse.

Day 258

Our interaction with God and our study of nature merge to inform and correct our interaction with our kin, first with our parents and siblings and later, if we become parents, with our own offspring. It can happen that the quality of relationship we could never create in our home of origin we can create in our own family. The pain and loss can stop with us and be replaced with nurturing kindness.

On this first natural life path we discover that a dynamic of mutual-influence can grow between two people who are genetically related that is uniquely rich in learning, discovery, and growth.

Sometimes we aren't aware of what we already know innately, deep inside, so we can't make much productive use of it. In a satisfying relationship with our kin, both of us discover innate tendencies and abilities with unusual clarity.

God has put living mirrors in our lives for a reason. Seeing ourselves in the reflexive, innate behavior of someone related to us else can provide feedback unlike any we can get anywhere else.

Day 259

Unlike the godless, we choose not to rush ahead to enjoy the benefits of relationships with people who are more removed, but rather to build our most immediate, constant, natural, and intimate relationships, as they are the ones most clearly given to us by God.

We don't substitute more distant and contrived relationships with many people for the more immediate and natural relationships we can have with the few people God already put in our lives.

The people we live with daily are those we know best who know us best. They know who we really are behind closed doors. They are the first to see what we do when we don't get what we want right away.

God is not a cosmic bookkeeper who runs a credit and debit system in which we can offset being selfish at home by being kind outside the home. This means we don't do nice things for a stranger outside the home, while treating our own parents, siblings, kids, or spouse unethically inside the home. We know that God is not fooled or impressed. God knows who we really are and so do they. We can see it in their eyes.

It is so clear in nature that God always goes for quality first over quantity. So do we, because we have learned that high-quality relationships have what it takes to make it into the future and low-quality relationships do not – no matter how many of them there are. The reason is simple. High quality relationships grow stronger under adversity. Low quality relationships collapse under adversity.

Day 260

We don't do nice things for strangers in our community or for a community halfway around the globe and think that absolves us from neglecting contact with God, learning from nature, caring for a parent, or from harming our child, partner, or sibling.

Neither do we seek clever ways to skim off resources intended for the larger community to enrich our own family at the expense of other families. We know God will not overlook and absolve such behavior.

Day 261

There is no absolution in nature, so we don't seek absolution from any human. In nature the only way to deal with having done something harmful is to unlearn the harmful behavior and replace it with helpful behavior.

We find no rigged games among social species in nature in which one creature always wins without first proving it is the most capable, and it can bring the most benefit to the group. Rather, in nature we see both complex symbiotic networks of mutual benefit and leaders whose authority is earned daily.

Among social species in nature, we do find self-dealers and clever gamers who take for themselves at the expense of the group. We also see that the group drives them off until they learn how to behave as constructive members of the group, not as parasites. Then they are welcomed back into the group to share in the benefits of voluntary cooperation.

Day 262

The doomed civilizations that have all come and gone were built on cheap substitutes and lazy short cuts, all aimed at quick and visible material prosperity, and all built on unnatural, unhealthy, and unequal family structures.

There are no short cuts to the regeneration, so we start where it all first went wrong to begin with and work our way outward from there, replacing any way of relating to each other based on coercion or manipulation with ways of relating based on fully informed consensus.

There are no substitutes, nor should there be, for the re-naturalizing work we must do for humanity to evolve to the point that our societies can be sustainable. Since each life pathway is from God, each relational pattern must be thoroughly re-learned and fully developed. Each pathway is a necessary building block we will use later to understand and build the next one.

Day 263

We were created to be stewards of and creative participants in something large, ancient, complex, and wonderful. It makes sense that we need to understand deeply the wonders that make creation wonderful and how they fit together.

Without deep humility and respect toward creation, we can't take good care of it all and go on to make contributions to make it all even better.

We avoid skillfully marketed shortcuts that promise faster results than those that come from initial failure, remorse, rethinking, relearning, and practice. History teaches us that shortcuts don't exist and using them hurls us into a mirage that ends in oblivion. The lessons about what not to repeat are there for us to learn and use to make better choices.

Day 264

Alluring, false promises of quick results on a grand scale attract the most energetic and ambitious among us. But in the long run they become disenchanted and bitter, blaming some other group for blocking their utopian or nostalgic dream of quick and easy prosperity. In bitterness and revenge former fanatics seek to dominate or even eliminate the group they blame for ruining the fantasy.

False promises set humans up for awful violent conflict in the future, because for every action there is an equal and opposite reaction, whether in physics or in politics. Since the earth is a shared space, we either live together creatively or die together horribly.

Day 265

True sustainability is about constantly renewing the living reciprocal systems within, between and around us. It is about recognizing, protecting, and nourishing the connections of mutual benefit between living things.

God uses nature as curriculum to teach us to see the whole, not just the parts we can take, manipulate, and use for our immediate benefit. We learn that over time, we benefit more from the healthy whole than we do from breaking things into parts and consuming them.

Day 266

There are two essential qualities found on any God-given, sustainable path:

Intimacy and accountability.

We look for these two qualities in deciding whether to participate. If these qualities aren't there we make changes to ensure both intimacy and accountability exist.

Intimacy means touching, being touched, staying in touch. When God is doing a work, we find we are in intimate, immediate, constant contact with real people and a real, local situation. Accountability means making sure our touch leaves what we touch unharmed, and if possible even better than it was before we touched it.

Day 267

God's rule only enters our lives through situations that are current and real. If we stay in constant touch with our real, current situation we will be in a position to see an opening only God could have created.

God's touch does not come to us when we fill our minds and lives with made up, soothing, entertaining, nonsense. Imaginary realities have always been the main ingredient godless humans use to avoid seeing the whole and to shut out the guiding ethical presence of God. Most religions and philosophies are specially designed to protect people from ever meeting God and to prevent the disruption of their selfishness that meeting God always brings.

We choose to reject and abandon these false, dead, and deadly systems. We don't live our lives sleepwalking through personal or collective invented fantasies, no matter how modern, ancient, or popular they are.

Day 268

We chose to engage reality instead of fantasy. A real situation is intimate, changing, and ambiguous, yet verifiable. Fanciful nonsense comes from someplace far removed and different from our direct personal experience. Fanciful nonsense is always a little too clear, unchanging and is impossible to verify directly. You're just supposed to turn off your brain and accept it. Fanciful nonsense is the specialty of con artists.

We know something is real because it directly touches our lives. A direct touch is the essence of intimacy.

What is real is also ambiguous, changing, confusing, contradictory, and messy. Yet what is real is also verifiable, measurable, observable, and testable over time.

Day 269

The defining features of what is real, when seen in combination, can be unsettling. We may feel a temptation to flee reality into an unambiguous and calming fantasy.

We resist this temptation for a reason.

Real knowledge we can use to solve problems is available as long as we are relating to reality itself with all its messy ambiguity, and constant change.

It takes time, but like any acquired taste, we come to prefer dealing with reality over dealing with fantasy. Only in reality, as opposed to fantasy, can we cooperate creatively with each other to make our real situation richer in natural diversity, with more happy surprising discoveries, more open to change, more complex.

Which is a way of saying we create a place that is fully alive. In such place we walk with God.

Day 270

We can't really learn anything about how to relate better to each other by studying the lives of people who weren't real, doing things they never did because they never lived. No creature in nature learns to thrive in a changing and challenging environment through escapism.

Leaving imaginary relationships to engage in real kin-relationships can be bracing at first, like jumping into a cold lake in the summer. But it can also be invigorating in a way that fantasy cannot.

Very few experiences are as real and messy as lifetime relationships with our kin. For instance, there are few things as full of messy uncertainty as parenting! Parenting never lives up to any ideal fantasy, but its rewards, which take decades to accrue, can make any imaginary story predictable and boring by comparison.

Day 271

To engage reality instead of fantasy we will need reliable information. If our life course has not provided us with the opportunity for first-hand experience with a particular topic, we seek out those who have had direct, first-hand experience to gain reliable information.

True expertise comes from having tried ideas to see how they work out over time. We can tell a real expert by the humility and humor that comes with multiple rounds of action-reaction feedback over extended periods of time.

Day 272

We create original combinations of insights from our own direct experience and that of others we know to be genuine experts. We test and improve our new combination with a series of careful experiments whose results we measure and acknowledge. In time, our results confirm that sustained direct engagement with what is real is useful, functional, and uniquely enjoyable.

God teaches us the difference between knowing general notions about something and really knowing something intimately for ourselves.

We develop a natural preference for intimate, hard-earned knowledge. A preference for solid information over hearsay does for humans what instinct does for other creatures. Being more discerning and perceptive fits us better to engage a changing future.

Day 273

In addition to intimacy, we find when God is doing a work through us, there is also accountability built into the relationships we are called to create and sustain.

Intimate contact with reality produces new ideas that can bear logical scrutiny. In a good relationship we must then answer for how true or false our ideas turn out to be. This sense of accountability causes us to correct and refine our ideas until we can consistently produce solutions that bear the weight of practical life.

Wise solutions must work as intended when they make contact with the real world. Foolish solutions collapse into absurd contradictions once they make contact with the real world.

God is never the author of foolish solutions.

Day 274

Accountability is reality-testing. We willingly subject our words and actions to penetrating logical and moral scrutiny. In a good relationship, if our actions don't match our words, we must look the person in the eye and answer for our hypocrisy. It is not an experience we wish to repeat!

We each grow and change until our actions surpass our words and our results are so undeniable words are no longer needed. It goes without saying.

If our results don't live up to our promises, we will have to answer for the failure, which can be documented in measurable terms. History, whether personal, institutional, or national is in large part a record of how things turned out compared to how popular or powerful people promised they would turn out.

God does not allow any institution to dismiss its historic and ongoing crimes by saying, "oh well, we're only human." Consistently denied and easily dismissed moral deficit is evidence that a population may be suffering from a particular form of degeneration - epigenic brain damage.

Day 275

As our instinctive wisdom grows through personal experience, it becomes easier to avoid getting on a path where we will not be met or helped by God. A false path in the future will lack either real intimacy or real accountability or both. There will be no daily interdependence with another real person in real time on equal terms. There will be no feedback to catch and correct uncooperative behavior as soon as it shows up.

Real intimacy is a kind of challenging love. False intimacy is a kind of easy love. An example is religions that create a god that is easy to love because the god is so forgiving and indulgent we never feel a need to tangibly and consistently improve how we treat each other.

False intimacy is imaginary closeness to an imaginary being, whether it be a god, a person, a theory, a fantasy world, or a celebrity. False intimacy is a kind of drug that makes us feel good about ourselves or our group before we have done anything to earn the right to feel good about ourselves. False intimacy masks the growing rot beneath the surface.

Day 276

We come to know God in a state of accountability for our behavior, or we don't come to know God as God at all.

It is not easy to love the true Creator because we can only make contact as long as we are actively identifying, abandoning, and replacing our harmful attitudes and behaviors as they come to our attention.

Real accountability is a kind of challenging stress test. If we have not built our lives or organizations God's way, they fall apart under the stress. If we have not built our work God's way it will disintegrate under stress.

Day 277

Pilots are responsible for the lives they transport. They have a saying…

"Fix it on the ground. Nothing ever gets better in air."

Before taking responsibility for the future of the earth, God will require that we identify and replace our own individual unethical attitudes, values, and behaviors and those of our group. We must do this before God will trust us to manage or intervene in the affairs of others beyond our own front door.

There is no reason to believe we will manage or intervene in the life of a larger group of people any better and any differently than the way we already manage and intervene in the relationships we have within the small group of people given to us. Larger influence does not mean better influence. Better influence means better influence.

Day 278

Until we can be trusted to take good care of the lives around us in the present, we will not be asked to do something that will take care of life on earth in the future. It is precisely what we learn to do differently right now that will lead us to discover new solutions to what lies in store for us in the future.

The answers we need are already embedded and waiting to be discovered in the solutions we must develop to solve the problems that already exist between us and others in our lives.

We fix it on the ground, and the fix is mostly ethical. The rest is practical.

To resolve both relational and practical problems we use solid, new information gained from direct contact with what is happening in our situation right here, right now. Only then does God call us to lift off the ground and fly into the future.

Day 279

A smug sense of intimacy with God without the discipline of accountability produces a kind of self-indulgent, religious spoiled brat. On this false path grows a sense of entitlement that produces religious tyrants who act like two-year-olds when they don't get their way.

At the other extreme, a tough sense of accountability without real loving intimacy with God produces anger, resentment, and a sense of never being good enough, no matter how hard we try. It is miserable to live with a thousand rules, constantly violating at least one of them.

To never feel acceptable or loved by one we deeply admire is to feel love-hate, the most destructive hate there is. It leads to rebellion, and eventually to the rejection of the very concept of God.

Day 280

Accountability does not mean living under a burden of guilt or shame. To see our relationship with God and nature that way is to distort a healthy, natural instinct.

God has high standards, but is not a vindictive, autocratic tyrant like those that have ruled vast, cruel empires. God is not an angry, resentful being who put us in debt at birth for the gift of life and then expects suffering and sacrifice to repay a loan we never signed up for. Over the course of history cunning priests create such debt/loan/sacrifice/repayment systems to lock in social status and a lifetime of passive income for themselves. God has nothing to do with such awful, dark, burdensome religious thought.

We don't fall for such lies. Instead, we return to the natural function of accountability.

Day 281

Accountability simply means that to participate in life on earth we must do so on life's terms, which were established billions of years before humanity emerged.

In nature we see living systems that are complex but form an integrated whole. We see evidence of tension and stress, but the system still endures and grows stronger. It is robust. It can absorb a shock and recover. We see evidence of wear, disease, and injury, but the system keeps repairing itself in such a way that it is still lovely to behold.

In God's design more does not mean more of the same. More means more differences and more combinations of differences.

Day 282

Being accountable to our Creator means we interact with creation in such a way that...

We keep the living systems we find intact while cultivating even more diversity...

We sustain the types of life we find and the connections that exist between them...

We make sure what we find remains just as robust as we found it and grows even more robust...

We see to it that the system loses none of its loveliness and gains even more in new and surprising ways.

When we treat what God created this way we come to live off the increase in the system, not off the slow death of the system.

Day 283

Any religious, economic, or political arrangement that violates life's terms, is built on lies and lies about God in particular. A false religious system will cause humans to resent, then reject God, then adopt technologies that harm life to live like parasites off the slow death of God's creation.

In contrast, any human arrangement that accepts life's terms and integrates itself into nature without harming it is true and good. A healthy, natural society will foster a natural longing to know God intimately by carefully observing the genius embodied in nature.

Day 284

We are constantly trying to find new, location-and situation-specific economic and political arrangements that God can happily endorse, support and protect. Politics is about how we solve problems that affect us all with solutions we can all live with. Economics is about how we will provide enough material support to everyone so they can fulfill the purposes God calls them to fulfill.

We know there will not be one political/economic arrangement that will fit every situation forever, but any arrangement we try we must be assessed against the requirement that it must preserve and increase life's wholeness, robustness, and beauty. Anything else and anything less is a crime in the eyes of God. God is just. Crimes bring their own penalty in the natural consequences they set in motion.

Day 285

We know that if our way of distributing power and material resources breaks apart combinations which must stay together to function, it conflicts with the way life works. It is not true to life and will not work. It will shut out the creative guiding and protecting presence of God.

We know If our way of solving our social and economic problems makes the living systems around us fragile and prone to collapse, it is untrue to life and God will not intervene to save what we have built. Rather, it will succumb to natural negative consequences.

If our way of meeting our social and material needs makes the living systems around us uglier, it is based in a lie about how life works.

We learn to monitor carefully and constantly how integrated, how resilient and how lovely our environment is. We change course immediately when we see the first signs of disintegration, instability, and any loss of its original attractiveness.

Day 286

How we will arrange our political and economic affairs now, here, in our shared situation today is an open mystery. Mystery is the name of a place that holds the answers we have not yet found. We naturally love a mystery. Mysteries are hard to resist.

Living creatively into a divine mystery is the most fulfilling way any human or human group can live. It is the way of living God designed for our species – nothing more, nothing less and nothing else will ensure our survival as part of earth.

It is in accepting and entering the open-ended mystery of our shared existence that we come to meet God as our Creator for the first time.

Day 287

To know God is to love and trust God. Only real intimacy with God, developed in silence and solitude, informed and inspired by nature- will cause us to willingly seek and welcome real accountability. Only this healthy stable combination of intimacy and accountability can restore both the name of God and bring the rule of God to earth, one soul at a time, one group at a time.

Only the rule of God on earth in each individual heart, and in local groups managing their local situation, can renew the earth and sustain humanity's catalytic role in the story of life for as long as our form of life is needed to fulfill God's mysterious purposes.

Day 288

Having learned how to cooperate with God, to learn from nature and to cultivate the potential creativity loaded into our own DNA and then the DNA of our kin, we can start down the next, natural relational life-path: friendship-partnership.

Once we know the value of both intimacy and accountability, we can form a relationship with someone who does not share our DNA but shares with us other things that are equally important. The ability to form a mutually-beneficial relationship with someone outside of our own family, and even outside our own species, is not unique to humans. We see this behavior in nature.

"Symbiosis" means to "live together." It means to share a space at the same time. When it works well, symbiosis makes the most of a space for as long as conditions permit. It often means improving the conditions both creatures find themselves in such that the environment can support a greater diversity of life.

Day 289

Having a true friend and partner is not just a passing experience. A true friend and partner constitutes a permanent, structural part of our lives. Such a relationship is a key structure we rely upon and build upon to do things we could not do on our own. There are tasks that are so large or complex that they can't be done alone. We can't be in two places at once. There are tasks that can only be accomplished by division of labor, with each person doing a different part of the work at the same time the other person is doing another part of the work.

A true friendship and partnership most often arises out of shared effort to achieve something that will benefit both people for a long time. A true friendship and partnership does not require being identical or agreeing on everything. In fact, the differences are a lot of what make the relationship useful and enjoyable.

Day 290

A stable, mutually beneficial partnership between two unrelated creatures of the same species provides a structure with the highest success rate in bringing something alive from infancy to full functional maturity – whether it be offspring, or a new idea.

Affection naturally grows between two creatures who both benefit from their relationship. So does empathy. It is natural to protect our partner/friend from harm if for no other reason, that their continued existence and well-being increases the odds of our own survival and happiness.

Day 291

We form and manage our non-kin, symbiotic relationships in the same way we manage our kin-relationship, for the same reason – to bring joy to God, which God returns to us, multiplied, in ways and at times we never could have foreseen.

We form a friendship/partnership to help each other figure out what is true and best, then put that information into action in the real world until it makes the world more just, increasing the stock of happiness on earth.

Day 292

Friendships that don't last or don't function well to solve problems were typically built on only shared pleasure or were formed just to gain an advantage to beat others in competition for resources or opportunity.

Pleasure friends must at least initially enjoy each other's company. Advantage partners don't even need to like being around each other and often don't.

When shared pleasure becomes boring, the friendship built on it quickly evaporates.

When someone becomes more of a burden than an advantage for any reason, a friendship built on gaining advantage becomes a disadvantage and it will be discarded and replaced, un-ceremonially, with astonishing speed. Those who build a friendship to gain an advantage also try to gain advantage over each other, leading to suspicion and distrust.

In short, pleasure and advantage relationships provide immediate gratification, but do not age well.

Day 293

Rather than build our lives around pleasure or advantage relationships, we form high-functioning partnerships with competent and reliable people who also seek God first and who also see the ethic of reciprocal helpfulness as primary and non-negotiable.

Having our shared loyalty to God as our deepest similarity, we can work together to pursue an ever-clearer understanding of reality, build a justice that includes more diversity, and create at least one useful innovation that those outside our friendship can use productively.

Day 294

These honorable, working relationships naturally turn into deep, lasting friendships. We don't pursue love. We pursue what honors God, which is whatever is true and good. Loving admiration grows between us as a natural by-product, each time we figure out together a new piece of the puzzle.

We sense our calling is to bring a good and true idea to life. We make the new idea viable for others by testing it ourselves individually and as a pair. We work the bugs out of it, resolving its contradictions. Like preparing a child to leave the nest, we equip the new idea to survive long enough to be a real, living alternative others can adopt.

Day 295

We learn through our creative journey that we can trust each other's competence and intent. Increasingly we include each other's well-being in our own sense of well-being. If our partner is doing well, we are doing well. If our partner is suffering, we are suffering too. Neither of us is alone in the adversities of life, or in the struggle to fulfill our calling.

We are there for each other when either of us really needs help, ready and willing to assist each other to do things that can't be done well alone or can't be done at all alone.

We have each other's back. We defend each other's interests and reputation when the other is not there, just as we do with God' interests and reputation, who is invisible and is apparently "absent" to those who do not seek God.

Day 296

The reason our friendship/partnership relationships last and remain fruitful is we form them to pursue something higher and build them on something deeper than pleasure or advantage.

Since we seek a friend/partner with whom we can build a life that honors God, we pair up with someone who is equal in capacity, but opposite in a few important ways, not opposite in everything. We are unified, but we are not copies of each other and have no need to agree on everything.

We look at and for the same thing, but from two different points of view. We correct each other's errors. We enhance each other's strengths.

We experience this healthy dynamic most vividly, most regularly in life partnerships, which are a special case of friendship. We also experience this dynamic in other friendships, especially when what we learn honors God at home we find we can apply in our other relationships.

Day 297

This equal-opposite design shows up everywhere in nature. Your eyes and ears lie on opposite sides of your head and use the different angle of reception to precisely locate things in space, even if the object is in motion. If you lay your right hand over your left they do not line up – they are mirror images of each other. If you turn your hands around and have them face each other – they can form a strong, stable, grasping unit. Your limbs have muscles that work in pairs – with one contracting, while the other relaxes, allowing smooth and controlled movement.

The result is the kind of graceful, careful action that only comes from power under precise, intentional voluntary control.

Day 298

How God does sustainability is about how we do anything we do. We don't have a plan; we have a way of relating. God's work of renewal is not about plans and strategies. It is about ethics. It is about how we treat each other and nature as we do anything we do.

Change is so constant that plans and strategies become obsolete very quickly. As finite mortal creatures, it is only our daily mode of engagement with reality that can be nimble enough to keep our actions relevant and constructive far into the future.

By following God's constant, daily ethical guidance at each point of decision that affects other lives, we find ourselves growing into the ability do the right thing together. We find ourselves doing the right thing, at the right time, in the right place, in the right amount, for the right reason without ever knowing ahead of time what form that right thing will take.

Forms, plans and methods come and go. Life's creative power and patterns remain.

Day 299

Our partnerships are formed to pursue the good and the true. To support this pursuit, we focus together on how we do things more than what we do. When God creates an opening, we know how to move smoothly through the opening. We know how to start something that would not have been possible otherwise. We know how to avoid dangers and make the most of opportunities.

"Know how" is where the action is. "Know what" is where the action was. God is always present where the action is, not where it was. Focusing on "how" questions more than "what" questions keeps us in a state of graceful movement.

In contrast, pleasure-based and advantage-based relationships end up in something more like a severe muscle cramp, with each part pulling with all its might against the other, trying to get what it wants at the expense of the other. The result is painful paralysis in the face of a situational challenge that imperils both parties. In this conflicted state, they cannot avoid dangers or seize opportunities, much less create something new, different, and better than anything that already existed around them.

Day 300

Through many rounds of practice, we travel farther on the God-given relational life path of non-kin partnership/friendship. Eventually we forge an effective, efficient team dynamic between us. The two of us have lived out a story that we share with no one else on earth or in history. That shared story that we wrote ourselves makes the two of us a "we" rather than a "you" and "me." Our partnership becomes central to our own sense of identity, worth and purpose.

It works only because we see the same few things as most important, but we approach them differently. It works because we each bring equal force to our efforts and arguments, while remaining completely committed to each other's well-being and to our shared, larger calling.

Day 301

A mature partner/friend relationship works only because each of us is all in.

Neither of us is half-hearted, indifferent, negligent, or incompetent in our area of expertise. We can count on each other to do our very best, which allows us to do our very best as a unit.

When God is honored in the founding, building, and maintaining of a relationship, then God is present in the daily experience of the relationship. Where God is present, differences are honored, developed, and linked together to build new and unique capacities.

A good functioning friendship/partnership makes tackling almost any situational challenge possible and makes eventual triumph more likely.

Day 302

The track record of our friendship/partnership speaks for itself. We find good, productive solutions to our shared problems far more often than not. Our issues rarely fester for decades. We find good solutions at higher rate than we used to because we never stop getting better at finding new solutions and putting them into practice. We find new and better solutions far more often than most people around us do – and they notice.

The cumulative result is a productive peace between us and all the benefits that come from it.

After several decades, we are usually not the pair with the biggest pile of cash. Yet in almost any gathering we are most often the pair with the safest, richest, most rewarding relationship. It shows. Others can see it in our eyes, our faces and in the elegance of our systems of behavior. When we are in the mix, disorder turns into lively order, conflict turns into surprising harmony, complaint turns into grateful contentment, despair turns into practical hope, emptiness turns into overflowing fullness.

It takes years to accrue, but we know first-hand true, lasting, satisfying richness. In God's way of living, delayed gratification is deep and lasting gratification.

Day 303

In nature, creatures avoid inbreeding because of the weakening genetic damage it causes. They partner with one of their own kind but not from their own family. They also look for a partner with strong, adaptive traits.

We do the same thing. We look for someone who agrees as to what is of highest importance – to find out what is true (not a lie) and do what is good (not what is dysfunctional). We seek someone who seeks God and honors the genius of God to be found in nature.

Yet we don't' stop there. We look for someone who is not a copy of us, who agrees with us on everything. Rather we seek someone who brings variety in both perspective and competence to the way problems can be approached.

We don't look for someone weak or weaker than us. We look for someone just as strong as us and stronger than us in some areas. No sane person wants a weak ally or to weaken a strong ally. A weak person may be easier to control, but they will be useless when danger or opportunity show up in the situation. A strong person can and will add something to any effort that we could not add on our own, just as we add something they could not add on their own.

Day 304

A strong partner will hold their own and stand their ground in an argument, only agreeing to do things differently when our own argument makes more sense – using observations and observable facts.

A strong and honorable partner will acknowledge a new truth revealed from examining the results of an experiment to test the merits of the two competing approaches. A strong creative partnership functions like the combination of muscles that power our limbs. They take turns pulling and releasing, contracting, and relaxing until the job is done. In like fashion, God designed the paring of two strong minds, two vigorous wills around shared commitment to discover what is true and good, regardless of what the culture advocates.

It is not an easy or fast process, but it is an effective one that delivers beautiful results when given enough time and attention. It takes strong people to see this through until the pattern of evolving excellence is clear enough that neither would want to live any other way. Weak people are too impatient to participate productively in this process.

Day 305

By building a productive, long-term non-kin partnership of any kind we learn more about how God does diversity. If the two partners were each represented by a circle overlapping in a Venn diagram the area of difference is roughly the same as the area of overlapping similarity.

Since both of us seek God and want to know what is good and true, we are similar enough to be stable. Having different family histories makes us different enough to keep things interesting and changing. Like all evolving creatures in nature, having a good partnership helps us make the most of the known, the new, and the combination of both.

Day 306

An example of a good working partnership would be the relationship between historians and archeologists. They are intellectual neighbors. Their disciplines are different, but they use a combination of similar and different research methods. They both want to know what the truth about what happened in the past, in part to understand how we got to where we are today.

Their larger research questions often overlap. They both respect each other and rely upon each other's work to make their own work better, often by correcting what was wrong or completing was incomplete. What is obvious at first glance for an archeologist is a stumper for the historian, and vice versa. Each eagerly anticipates new discoveries from the other. In this way knowledge does not just grow in quantity, it gets better in accuracy, leading to better, more fruitful questions – which renews and restarts the learning process over again.

As they work historians and archeologists interact with each other without interfering with each other. That is what it means to participate. No coercion is needed to motivate their work because it is natural to seek the opportunity to fully participate in something real, alive, unfolding, and wonderful.

Day 307

God does sustainability by creating real partnerships. Real partnerships do not involve coercion. All efforts are fully voluntary. Since it is a form of coercion, God does not use guilt or any sense of debt to motivate. Guilt produces compliance at best, but forced compliance produces resentment and cunning ways to cheat over time.

God uses fear of natural consequences to make us careful not to harm ourselves or others, but God does not use fear of punishment to motivate. Fear of punishment can produce compliance but over time it produces paralyzed numbness as people just go through the motions with no passion or commitment.

Living in fear is no way to live. We need to have enough realistic fear to stay away from what can harm us and others, but any more fear than that takes more from us than it gives in return.

Day 308

Partnerships built on greed quickly descend into conflict when one partner seems to gain more from the arrangement than the other.

Greed, pride, and envy can stimulate temporary surges of commitment and creativity. The fastest way to get rich and famous is to create something that appeals to human vanity, laziness, and selfishness, but most often the result is an improved, easier, faster way to achieve something that is not good to achieve.

Any human achievement that displaces the sense of dependence on God's guidance, the sense of interdependence with each other, and the sense of accountability for how we treat nature is a step closer to extinction.

To ensure partnerships are healthy, and that the resulting work does no harm to earth, God does not use greed, pride, or envy to motivate each partner's efforts.

Day 309

Instead of guilt, fear, greed, pride or envy, God uses the simple natural desire to participate to motivate.

It is natural to want to join in and experience for oneself what it is like to do what other creatures are already doing or have done in the past, both human and otherwise.

Watch a baby who is about to start crawling or talking and you can see how much she wants to do what is naturally next for her to do. She has no problem motivating herself. She knows it can be done and wants to do it because she sees others already can do it.

God designed us to feel this innocent childlike desire to participate in what is naturally next for the entire course of our lives. This is the joy of living. It is the mainspring of our passion for life. It is enough to sustain or efforts through all our natural social obligations because in fulfilling our social obligations God touches us and renews our love of life, as only the author of life can do.

Day 310

God does not meet us in contrived, unnatural roles and obligations motivated by guilt, fear, greed, pride, or envy. A life lived apart from God's regularly surprising touch is a living death.

The desire to participate can keep us healthy and happy for a lifetime, because God renews this desire every day. Any other form of motivation peters out and eventually curdles into a poison that deadens us and those around us.

Day 311

A calling is a sense we have deep inside that in time we will be able to participate in a particular way. The healthy, natural desire to participate calls us to contribute something new that will interact with what God has already created in such a way that it gets even better, more interesting, and more fruitful.

To participate is to take part in something, to share in something larger than ourselves, something that already exists and operates on its own terms.

Day 312

God does not ask us to beat ourselves up, do penance or offer sacrifices to atone for the things we have done wrong. There is no donation we can make that evens out our harmful deeds. Rather, we take our sense of guilt, which is healthy, and seek God to learn what to do with it.

We had no business disrupting God's natural distribution system. What would have been created will never be created because of what we did. It is lost forever. Why should our sense of grief go away? The loss has not gone away. Our violation is against God. We feel guilt because we are guilty.

When we take our guilt to God, what God requires, to our surprise, is that we simply stop doing what we have been doing and start learning to participate in life on life's terms as part of earth - today. If we have done harm God directs us to restore what we have harmed, to give back what we took that was not ours to take, because it was something God gave to the ones we harmed for a divine purpose. We have no right to disrupt a divine purpose.

The feeling of guilt serves to keep us from doing more harmful things in the future. It is a gift from God to protect the fullness of life from any further harm. We honor it. We don't try to relieve ourselves from it. Our example of new, helpful behaviors inspires the young to choose better behaviors than the harmful ones we chose in the past.

Day 313

As we do more new things that are in keeping with God's expectations, there is a change in how much harm we have done to life versus how helpful we have been to life. The more consistently helpful we have been, and the longer we have lived that way, the better we can feel about how we have used the freedom of choice God gave us.

We naturally start to forget what that was like and have no desire to go back. Healthy forgetting is a wonderful kind of natural buoyancy that frees us *from* dark heaviness and frees us *for* even more useful participation in life on life's terms. We are changed, and then we can go from living in a cycle of shame to living in a cycle of joy.

Day 314

The way God designed it, tragedy is not the basis of life. The fear of death is not the basis of true religion. Alienation is not the basis of creativity.

The desire for simple, joyful, playful, spontaneous, daily, trusting participation – that is the basis of life. Participation in life requires faith enough to listen and learn the rules of life from the Author of life. Participating requires listening obedience to an intelligence beyond our own. That is all true religion is. Belonging to the community of life and wanting to enrich the experience of all lives in that community is the basis of creativity.

We are drawn deeper into life by a kind of magnetic desire, not pushed through life by some kind of monstrous fear. We don't spend our lives fearing death or trying to secure a life after death with some religious gimmick. God created death as a natural and a necessary part of life. Without death there would be no space available for new lives on earth. What God creates is good.

One life is plenty if we are really living.

Day 315

The thing we truly fear is not really living while living the only life we get. It is a natural, protective healthy fear given to us by God, like the fear of heights.

We fear not participating – as well we should. God only gives us a handful of natural, healthy fears but they are there to protect us. The fear of not participating is one of them. When we don't participate in the life of earth on life's terms we are doing things that life can't support. Or we are not doing the things that life can support. Either way our activities are unsustainable and will culminate in sudden collapse, slow extinction, or both.

In time as we listen and follow, God relieves the very fears God gave us for our protection by teaching us behaviors that move us out of harm's way. We find the closer we live to God, the closer our actions resemble the way nature solves problems, the more helpful and cooperative we are with each other – we need not fear missing out on full participation in the miracle of life. Our daily experience is more than enough to bring happiness and often more than we can fathom or put into words.

As full participants in life there are moments when only laughter, song and tears of joy can express what we feel. Otherwise, we would be dumbstruck with awe.

Day 316

God's happiness is about participating productively in a working relationship with God and nature. Good relationships are ones that accomplish something - something that would not have been possible or at least would have been extremely difficult to do without the relationship.

The best way to accurately predict that someone from your "neighborhood," someone who shares your frame of reference will make a good partner - is to see them work. Then to examine their work. We often first learn the person exists by reputation - someone we already know, and trust has seen the person work and examined their work.

In contrast, if you can't admire the way someone works or the quality of their work, you can't form a productive non-kin relationship with them. Never overlook shoddy work. Never make excuses for it. Move on. Keep looking. When you need a new relationship to get something done you are called to do, God will provide without asking you to lower your standards.

Day 317

Remember, whereas kin-relationships are largely mandatory – non-kin partnerships are voluntary. We can't choose our family, but we can choose our friends and partners, and those choices define us and go on to either constrain or expand our options later in life.

Since the stakes are so high, as we seek and choose long-term friendships and partnership, we seek God at every step along the way. We look for someone we can admire for a lifetime, someone with whom we can continue an interesting conversation for a lifetime. We look for ways to see a potential partner's work, to see them working because that tells us more about who they really are than anything else besides their friend group.

Always look at who they are friends with. That group is where they feel they belong because that is what they think they are. Good company makes everyone better who shares it. Bad company makes everyone worse who shares it.

Day 318

There are warning signs we must not ignore when selecting a lifetime friend or partner. If we can't talk about God and God's priorities with the person we can know ahead of time we can't partner with them without losing the presence of God in our lives and God's guidance in our work.

Imagine how offensive it would be to a wife if her husband befriended a man who routinely speaks with vulgar contempt about women in general and his own wife in particular.

We see things from God's perspective. We realize that it is deeply offensive to God when we give the solace of friendship to someone who denies God or God's rights in the affairs of humans. We don't expect God's help when we live in a way that is offensive to God.

Day 319

We become more like those we spend a lot of time with. Over time the quality of our lives matches the average quality of our long-term friends, co-workers, and partners. The fastest way to raise the quality of our lives is to avoid on-going relationships with those who do not believe they are accountable to God for their actions.

The best way to sustain growth into an ever-higher quality of living is to cultivate and protect relationships with those who know they are accountable to God for their actions.

Whenever possible we seek to cultivate mutually beneficial relationships with those who surpass us in some helpful set of abilities.

Day 320

We learn from those we spend time with. If we spend time with those who consistently fail to create more well-being around themselves, we are learning from those with failed values. And from them we can only learn how to fail.

This is especially true when it comes to our relationship with existing institutions. If an institution has promised for centuries to make the world a better place, but has never done so, - to learn what that institution has to teach is to learn how to replicate and extend its failure for another generation.

Learning to fail from those who keep failing is a waste of time, energy, and attention. If we seek God's direction and correction God will not allow us to be so wasteful. If we ignore God's direction and correction and proceed to live wastefully it is impossible to escape the consequences forever.

We have the courage to walk away and learn God's wisdom from nature, plus our own direct experience plus the messages we receive from our own conscience. We finally see that by walking away we have not lost a relationship; we have lost the illusion that we ever had a functioning relationship in the first place. All we have lost is a losing relationship. Like patching a leak in a tire, losing a constant source of loss is to achieve a solid win.

Day 321

Loss is part of life as God designed it. The ability to recover from loss is a critical ability that allows us to live sustainably, both individually and collectively.

Individuals who can't recover quickly from loss form groups that also can't recover quickly from loss. Groups built to avoid risk also resist change because they have no ability to recover from the loss change will bring. In turn such groups create new individuals who cannot recover quickly from loss – and the vicious cycle repeats itself, drawing in and sucking down more and more people. If our central value is avoiding loss we can't be co-creators with God.

Among us, God has set up a new virtuous cycle. An individual who cultivates the ability to recover quickly from loss to become even more creative and productive will create a partnership than can do the same. Partnerships can expand into larger groups that can collectively recover from loss. These larger groups produce individuals who think it is normal to recover from loss quickly and creatively.

In history, the way culture changes for the better is when a small group of people creates a new, better way of living and others start to copy it. The new way spreads naturally by imitation and modification, solving old, unsolved problems and creating new opportunities.

Day 322

When God makes something it has three characteristics that cumulatively can be described as flourishing. When something is flourishing in nature it forms an integrated whole, it is resilient, and it is a feast to the senses.

Any religion, economic or political system that does not take good care of and unify all its parts is unsustainable. A system that lacks natural wholeness will not respond quickly to change and loss, while still caring for all its members. A system unable to make necessary changes when it is time will be ugly to watch in operation, leaving something that is repulsive to the senses. Such systems are not from God and are doomed to inevitable, irreversible extinction.

We do not "go along to get along" with godless human inventions. We will not be complicit in the harm to life such a system inflict. We protest. We reform. We say "this cannot be true. This is not good; clearly this does not work. We will no longer participate. We will keep looking, under God's guidance for better ideas and then test them with experiments. We will honestly evaluate the results of our experiments against God design criteria: wholeness, resilience, and a wonder to behold in action. In nature something is a wonder to behold because if we pay close attention we see high order that keeps moving toward even higher order.

Day 323

When God calls, changes, and rebuilds an individual from the inside out that person will evolve a peaceful integrated personality. God's signature mark of wholeness shows itself in a life that is peaceful, resilient, and nimble. God-made nimbleness is beautiful to observe in operation, leaving a legacy of higher, more functional social norms to emulate and extend.

Such individuals naturally build partnerships, families and other human groupings that are also unified while retaining their differences. These partnerships are creative and nimble in response to loss and change, and a quiet wonder to observe when solving any problem together, creating anything new together. Godly groups leave in place flexible, elegantly simple solutions others can safely imitate and improve upon.

Day 324

Godless worldlings are often wildly creative, but not ethical. Their creations destroy what is not theirs to destroy, but rather something held in common with others. Something is held in common when it comes from, is done by or shared by more than one. Ungodly creativity treats something held in common as if it is private, coming from, done by and belonging to one individual or group. This is unethical and ultimately doomed behavior.

Another version of unnatural creativity is to be book-bound in their ethics, using a long set of rules, but not practically creative in timely response to loss and change. Leaving one's community paralyzed and rigid when action is required is also unethical and ultimately doomed behavior.

God's standard is to be ethically and constantly creative.

We never choose between ethics and creativity. If we live inside a religion, an economic system and a political structure that is natural and from God ethics and practical creativity will be two sides of the same coin. Ethical creativity takes care of what is held in common first and foremost and then responds to change in ingenious new adaptations. Separating ethics and creativity is as unnatural as trying to separate the light of the sun from the warmth of the sun. If you get one you get the other eventually. If you lose one, you lose the other eventually.

Day 325

If something made by humans breaks up the wholeness of nature, and/or makes natural systems non-resilient, and/or makes a natural system stunted and uglier than was before, then we turn away from it and face the unknown. We seek the undiscovered solution known only to God but already modelled somewhere in nature.

If something made by humans hollows out the human soul and turns humans against or away from each other into warring groups, if it produces individuals who are rigid and unable to change, if it produces ugly attitudes and behaviors, then we turn away from it and turn toward the unknown. God has a better way to be human individually and collectively. God's way is as natural and effective as the way trees grow and interact with each other in a healthy forest. We are called to find God's ways of doing things.

Day 326

Only ethical and creative human endeavors are sustainable. Activities that are only one without the other will be popular and will expand rapidly out in space across the globe but will not extend out in time beyond a generation or two at most. A popular fad will be replaced by the next popular fad. A rigid tradition will be abandoned by young people born into it who find it boring and irrelevant.

Activities that are ethical and creative have what it takes to extend out in time, far beyond our individual lifetimes. However, these new norms will not be popular today, nor will they have what it takes to expand rapidly out to govern more space across the globe. When God starts something new and better it is always hidden, hyper-local and very small, but it is good and true. What God starts spreads only by natural attraction and voluntary imitation, not through sales, marketing, or through bribes and government threats.

Day 327

Uniquely among other creatures, humans have the ability to store and pass on information. Information passed on is what makes things happen that would not have otherwise happened or prevents things from happening that would have otherwise happened.

Tradition is the name for this storing and passing on of information from mind to mind, from generation to generation. We don't have the option of having no tradition. Our only option is to have a functional one that keeps getting better or a dysfunctional one that doesn't get better in response to new discoveries and experiences.

Refusing to change when change is warranted is a feature of dysfunctional and destructive tradition.

Day 328

Our tradition is to uphold the way God designed life to flourish. God's way is to constantly update our understanding of how life endures and flourishes, then incorporate our new understanding in the way we live and manage our affairs together.

There is one thing we refuse to change. We refuse to abandon our way of engaging in constant learning from direct contact with God, with nature, with history, with reality, and with each other. We refuse to stop or cheapen the never-ending process of ethically guided, cooperative innovation, in response to a constantly changing environment.

Our unchanging tradition is to keep changing under God's direction.

Living this way, we are never bored, and life is never empty or tedious. Wonders never cease to enter our minds and lives and make their way into our work.

Day 329

What we see in a natural habitat that has not been disrupted by human activity is autonomous flourishing. The living system we see maintains and grows itself, without inputs from outside itself. It has done so for a long time through all sorts of calamities. It somehow continues to exist. It stands on its own living base and that base is deep and rich enough to support it.

We don't rush through a natural living system, using it simply as decorative or therapeutic wallpaper as we focus on ourselves, our concerns, and ambitions.

Instead, we slow down, fall silent and observe any flourishing natural system. When we do this we feel the natural, gentle longing to take part in what we see, not to dominate it, exploit it or change it to make ourselves more comfortable. We feel humbled. We sense in such a space we are the students, and this living system is teacher as wise as it is ancient.

Where natural flourishing combines with the human desire to participate in a healthy way, it feels natural to take only what we need to survive and grow, then to give back as much or more than we took so other lives can survive and grow alongside ours.

Day 330

Living systems use no more than the energy the sun gives daily plus the stored pockets of that energy that were created within the lifespan of the creatures that live there. Living systems do not tap energy that was stored millions of years ago. We heed this example and keep working to find ways to build a new society that also does not need to use ancient, stored energy, which when burned, alters the atmosphere.

In living systems each species maintains its own population by balancing how many young it produces with how much energy it can secure from current sources to feed its young. We heed this example and keep working to create a cooperative society in which individuals flourish and contribute more to the stock of happiness we all share. A larger stock of happiness encourages enough of us to have enough children to maintain our population. We find enjoyment seeing them flourish as they discover who God made them to be so they can fulfill the calling God has for them.

Day 331

Because of the costs involved, neither live-long partnership nor parenthood should be entered into lightly, on a whim.

We seek God's guidance about whether to start a family, and how many children to have. Some of us willingly have larger families. Some of us have smaller families. Some of us have no children. Some of us live alone if that is what makes the most sense for us. Somehow God makes sure there are enough of us to sustain our population without anyone feeling coerced into marriage or parenthood.

Resentful compliance cannot generate enough effort to support effective parenting for decades. With all its struggles, frustrations, inconveniences and costs, the role of parenting must be chosen freely without any kind of coercion because it is a decades-long work of loving commitment.

Since we cooperate to provide support and enrichment for all the children God has entrusted to our community, our parents don't feel overwhelmed and alone in the struggle. Our cooperation cuts the burden of parenting dramatically and multiplies the joys of parenting because we all celebrate the flourishing of any child who grows up among us.

Day 332

Long-lived species contribute more to life on earth as a whole than they extract to survive. They deserve to persist.

Until we want to live within the energy budget given to us by the sun today and over the past 20 years or so, we will live beyond our means. We won't deserve to persist. Once we want to live within our means and have worked out a way to do so, we will deserve to persist. We don't know how to get there ahead of time, but we know the One who does know. We will have to change from the inside out and only God knows how to bring that about. In a regenerating state we can become a healthy, integral part of nature, just as God designed us to be.

Day 333

Until parents genuinely enjoy raising more than two children, because they experience rewards that more than offset the taxing effort they put in, we won't deserve to persist as a society or a species.

If parents feel alone, unvalued and abandoned it is unjust to expect them to bear the burden of our long-term survival. If our solutions to our collective challenges don't work for any of us, or for only one gender at the expense of the other, they won't work for all of us. This is why we don't set up gender or class-based dominance structures that impose costs of some with no real rewards and give rewards to others who bear no real costs. We insist on sharing power and burdens equally as we find solutions to any shared existential threat.

Once we have created a way of living together that makes bearing the burden of parenting for decades a reasonable activity, because there are both short term and long-term rewards for doing so, we will finally deserve to persist.

We don't know how to get there, but we seek the One who does know. We bring the question, heavy hearted, to God and listen, ready to change whatever we must change to respond.

Day 334

The root cause of unsustainability is insubordination. We are not God yet function as if we are. We do not know what is best but function as if we do. We spend no time or effort knowing God as God. We only seek God as a last resort to get us out of bind so we can go back to our insolent attitudes and avoid consequences for our insubordinate actions.

The root cause of sustainability is willing subordination to a Creative Mind greater than our own, fulfilling the desires of God's heart which has a capacity for kindness beyond anything we can imagine. So, we don't attach to notions or plans or theories. As living beings, we attach to a Living Being.

We are not in charge and don't know what we're doing. If we sever or reject a trusting, obedient, nimble working relationship with God, then we will get it wrong every time even if our intentions are good. We can't predict the future because there are so many more variables in play than any finite mind can grasp.

Day 335

To achieve sustainability, we don't need new answers. We need a new relationship with our Creator, with creation and with each other. The new answers we find will come as natural byproducts of the cluster of virtues we use to maintain and grow our relationship with God, nature, and each other.

Because the only thing that does not change in the universe is change itself, we attach our minds and hearts directly to God and find our home in nature. God's goodness and wisdom will never go away. The more we come to understand the genius embedded in life, our understanding of that goodness and wisdom will unfold in surprising ways we can't predict or control.

Since our desire now is to participate, not to possess, control and exploit, we have no fear of missing out on the best that can be.

Day 336

Many humans have mistakenly thought that accepting our limits and choosing subordination to God means giving up freedom. It does not. It means giving up foolish, destructive freedom and accepting wise, constructive freedom. False freedom is the license to do whatever we want. True freedom is the ability to achieve excellence.

Just as a bird is free to do amazing things in the air only because it obeys the laws of aerodynamics, doing the work to master the disciplines of any craft frees you to do things later you could not have done or even conceived without those disciplines. Ask any musician or artist. True freedom leads to levels of creative achievement beyond anything we imagined before learning the disciplines.

The creative solutions to our energy and population problems are like the acrobatics a bird finds it can do once it has learned to fly. The answers to the sustainability riddle lie within the zone of changing ambiguity we fear and have not yet entered. The motivation to find these answers comes from the longing for living connection God which already embedded in our bodies.

Will we accept constructive freedom and do the work to find these answers? It remains to be seen. But its beginnings are already there, hidden from sight in the heart of some who have always seen things differently than the crowd, and who have a price for it.

Day 337

A social Creator created us to be social creatures, defined by the beautiful elegance of our daily interactions with God, nature, and each other. The way we interact is effective - it solves problems and creates new unforeseen possibilities. The way we interact is efficient - it does not waste lives or resources doing things that reverse themselves into nothing.

Our actions are effective and efficient because we see ourselves as part of a whole, working to make the whole better. We don't see ourselves as apart from the whole, trying to grab everything we can for ourselves no matter the harm to others.

We see other lives as part of our life. We see our lives as part of the lives of others. We see and feel their pain or joy inside our bodies as our own pain and our joy. We offer the response we would need ourselves at such a moment, to reduce the pain or to expand the joy. This way of seeing our own lives limits our actions to only those actions God will support and enrich.

Day 338

Paradoxically, when we accept God's ethical limits on our behavior we set in motion solutions that are much less limited in time. They start small but last. This means we must have the courage and patience to quietly inhabit a small area of influence for now. What is crucial is not how well known we are, but how well-functioning we are.

Godly solutions to the challenges posed by life on a changing planet have a unique quality; the built-in ability to sustain themselves far into the future, becoming ever more beautiful, effective, and efficient.

Actions that are not ethically limited start big and loud but peter out into silent nothingness.

Day 339

God-directed and limited behavior will move us into a zone of untapped possibilities, pregnant with an unborn sustainable human society. It is both a play place and workspace. When we approach the sublime, the presence of The Creator at work, what we enter is like a large, open artist's studio where artists working in different mediums work alongside each other and inspire each other, bathed in natural light from large windows open to a natural space.

God's studio opens to us once we have learned to live in a state of disciplined play within God's ethical limits. There we aspire to nothing less than living up to the high standards set by nature's masterpieces of cooperative flourishing. We have mirror neurons that naturally cause us to imitate the behaviors we see around us. For instance, if we turn our attention to trees we will start to become more like trees, which survive and thrive by supporting each other.

In any working studio, all the artists get better if there is one that is better than all the rest, especially if that one is gracious and approachable.

Day 340

The solutions God will guide us into will be found on the frontier, where the known ends in complete perplexity, and where the unknown and unexplored begins. It is on the frontier that the limits of the human mind meet the limitlessness of God's mind. We have arrived at the true final frontier. We will not go there in shiny new spaceships. We will go there in new relationships, built to last.

On the frontier we don't find all the luxuries humans think they need to be happy. On the frontier we find how little we really require to be happy and whole. To our surprise, we find we can live full lives in a state of elegant simplicity, lives that are both functional and beautiful.

Well-designed studios have all the tools artists need but are not cluttered up so much that there is no place to try new things. In God's frontier studio there is nothing missing that flourishing requires. There is nothing extra to block our view of nature, nothing to clog the flow of creative flourishing from God's mind through our lives and out to create a new sustainable society.

Day 341

In the zone of divinely guided discovery, we learn to love our place in creation. Here we can find joy through all the natural passages in the journey, often emerging from the pain and loss that is part of all lives everywhere.

Here we discover there is something uniquely wonderful about each stage of life, even as each has its own limitations, challenges, and frustrations.

By listening to each other and learning from each other, we help each other make the most of the potential advantages each stage offers, while minimizing the real and potential disadvantages of each stage. We are there for each other through them all, adjusting to each other's legitimate needs as they change with age.

Day 342

God's frontier community is a wonderful place to be born, to grow up, to start a home, to raise a family, to rise to the peak of our powers, to lead when called upon to do so.

Because of the way we treat each other it is also a safe place to decline, to hand the reigns to the next generation, and to age well, passing on information that will live again in the actions of those yet to be born. We don't perish into nothingness. Through embodied wisdom we pass as models into the future. In this way we live again in new lives creating new endeavors that honor God and are honored by God's living presence.

The creative zone ruled by God is the best place to finally die, knowing we have done our best to increase the stock of holy happiness available to the lives we shared space with all along the way. Our passing is marked with heartfelt expressions of admiration and gratitude and with earnest promises to continue in some form our legacy of excellence.

Day 343

Ordinary mystery is a known, temporary, and limited space comprising a list of things we know we don't yet understand. This list creates another list of things we don't yet know how to build and operate. Powered, controlled flight was once such a mystery. We didn't understand the very real but invisible forces acting on a wing, so we did not know what kind of machine we needed to respond to those forces. Now we understand the dynamics of flight, and put that understanding to use to design, build and operate aircraft. Mystery solved.

There are ultimate mysteries that share a boundary with ordinary mysteries but go beyond them. An ultimate mystery is about what we don't yet even know we don't know. These mysteries dwarf any human mind, and all human minds combined.

Sustainability is one of the ultimate mysteries, and may be *the* greatest mystery, because it is open-ended. It will never stop being a mystery because we can't foresee the changes coming around the corner that will require new, sustainable responses from humanity.

Day 344

Sustainability is about living on into an unknown future and thriving there despite everything that has the power to extinguish life.

Sustainability is life participating in the eternal, infinite, unlimited life of God. Sustainability will not and cannot arise from a fixed set of answers, because it is impossible to anticipate every question that will one day require an answer.

Sustainability will only arise from an ever-evolving system of mutually beneficial interactions. Sustainability is a relationship. A love relationship.

Day 345

There is only one way to enter the mystery of sustainability. It is to be in a state of trusting, learning, adjusting, completely devoted and daily renewed intimacy with God – The Infinite Mind. Without this state of intimate connection, outside the condition of sustained "withness" we will forever be barred from participation in creating what will turn out to be sustainable.

Sustainability is not about what you know, it is about Who you know – the One who already knows everything, including everything about you. Rather than know everything before we trust anything, we trust the One who knows everything as the means to knowing what we need to know. Not just individually, although it starts there and is sustained there.

Day 346

There is an overflowing fullness that comes from being with God, living in a state of "withness" that is completely beyond the reach of those who do not seek God and admire nature. In God's fullness we are content. We don't need to live in the constant state of complaint that causes us to constantly grab and destroy more of the natural world.

The "fullness of withness" means living with God, with nature, with each other in a state of mutual protection, support, and nurture. This state of "withness" is the secret to sustainability. We enter the mystery of sustainability individually, then collectively. It is in learning a new way to treat each other that we uncover the insights God has already placed there for us; information we will use to build a new sustainable society, rising like the phoenix, from the ashes of the old society that could not save itself.

Day 347

Sustainability is not only about Who you know. Even more it is about Who really knows you as you really are today. God is the only one who knows that you can and will actually do and do well. God is the only one who knows that your social unit can and will actually do and do well. None of us are the best judge of our own capabilities. We hide too much from ourselves and from each other, but we can hide nothing from God. God hides insights and withholds tasks from those who will not allow divine inspection and correction.

Getting to participate in the work of sustainability starts with fully trusting God but shifts into active mode only when we have proven ourselves trustworthy to God. Trustworthiness qualifies us to be entrusted with divinely given and guided work.

We commit our lives to become one of those to whom God can safely delegate whatever needs to be done daily, knowing it will get done well, on time, and completely.

Day 348

To be trustworthy to God is to be fully available to God's fluid will. God is timeless and any delegated task from God will share in that timelessness. Humans have been around for at least 150,000 years, living in groups, adapting to the natural environments they found as they migrated out of Africa and into every continent. Humans began settling down and building cities about 10,000 years ago.

If a way to access God's constant guiding presence didn't exist until humans invented cities, palaces, and temples, that means humans were cut off from God for over 140,000 years.

Would God have left a sentient, curious, learning, inventing species with no way to experience living cooperation with its Creator for that long?

Of course not.

Day 349

The kinds of behaviors and tasks God delegates to those who are trustworthy today are the same kinds God delegated to trustworthy humans in the distant past - long before cities came into being with all their mysterious priests and exalted rulers.

They are the same behaviors and tasks God will delegate to trustworthy humans in the distant future. There is a simplicity and timelessness about what God directs us to do and not do.

We can well afford to remove all the bloated pageantry that only served to distract our attention away from our real obligations to life. We will not miss it.

God directs us away from behaviors and tasks what are not sustainable because they serve no purpose that is useful to life.

What is left is sustainable. Seeking, sensing, and following God's direction away from harmful ideas and activities is what makes us trustworthy.

Day 350

Trustworthiness is about being available, receptive and response to constant direction from the inside. Receiving direction is a function of felt closeness. We can feel the pleasure of God as our actions embody God's priorities, and as we learn to synchronize our lives with God's actions.

Conversely we feel the distance of God when we don't embody God's priorities or synchronize our lives with God's actions.

We feel the safety of directing closeness by removing all the distractions, barriers, and blockages between ourselves and God, both individually in social units of two or more.

Day 351

It is not possible to remain close to God while trusting and praising anyone or anything else more often than God. Removing blockages and rivals to God is like opening the ceiling to the sky above, letting in the full force of the sun into the courtyard of our souls and the plaza of our society.

Finally, everything new and unprecedented begins to grow again in its own way. All of God's waiting creations combine to form a wonderful place to live, a place where God feels welcome among us. In this unblocked and open space, to our delight and surprise, we often feel the presence of God filling our hearts and the space between each other.

Day 352

God will only entrust the work of renewal and sustainability to a people who have already proven themselves to be trustworthy. What we have already done that others have not sets us apart as trustworthy. What we have already stopped doing that others are still doing is what proves we can be trusted to not harm anything new God wants to create.

Staying so close to God that we can feel a nudge and hear a whisper has moved us out of the culture and closer to nature, where we can study God's role models of creative sustainability more closely and constantly.

Day 353

We now live on the margins of the doomed society in small numbers. Standing on principle and insisting on ethical solutions to practical problems has moved us up to higher ground. We stand for something beyond and above ourselves and others know it. Here, near the peaks, we find enough to just sustain ourselves.

Here we stand. We stand up for what is right and best. We are still here despite the efforts of all those who have tried to deny us a space on earth. We listened, obeyed, and were sustained through everything so we could hold this ground.

Day 354

In nature, it is the rare creature that has survived catastrophe that goes on to trigger a cascade of evolution resulting in a new and different ecosystem in which it thrives.

The current size of something does not predict its long-term success. In fact, the opposite can be true. The larger something is the faster it collapses and the shorter its time on earth. The smaller something is, the nimbler and more adaptable it is. It requires fewer and more diverse resources to survive, so it is less likely to collapse, so it has a longer tenure on earth.

In nature a large population often burns through all the resources it needs to sustain itself. Large populations often have become overly dependent on just one resource to the point that they cannot function at all without it.

In human history, large dominant powers have been very bad at self-assessment, dramatically underestimating their vulnerabilities and overestimating their strengths.

Day 355

In nature it is the small, somewhat lonely, scattered population that takes advantage of its situation and finds ingenious adaptations that allow it to use fewer and more sporadic resources. These adaptations allow it to survive when any one resource goes away because it can quickly shift to another one.

In human history, smaller powers on the margins of great powers have been much better at self-assessment. They more accurately estimate their vulnerabilities because it is impossible to overlook them. They more accurately estimate their strengths because they did not inherit them for free, they built up their strengths on their own since no one else was going to do it for them. Afterall, no one else thought they were worth the effort.

Day 356

There is an added bonus to small-scale local self-sufficiency. When you build something yourself you also know how to fix it, maintain it, modify it, or move it when necessary. Quick recovery is essential to survival when the catastrophe arrives.

We may not be much to look at today but here is a stubborn fact: we are still here. We are the remnant. We are the seeds of a new civilization. We may look dormant, but we are alive and waiting in the wings of history.

We are seeds divinely designed to germinate after the great fire.

Day 357

A great fire is coming. The fire of war, the war for more of what is left as every natural resource dwindles from overuse and mismanagement. The great fire will remove all that was unsustainable, everything built from decisions that never should have been made, turned into actions that never should have happened. It was also unsustainable because it omitted a few decisions that should have been made and turned into actions that should have happened.

The ratio is about 70/30.

Seventy percent of the failure stemmed from complicated nonsense that must never again take hold. Thirty percent of the failure stemmed from ignoring a few simple truths that must be honored and enacted.

Day 358

We know by heart the list of actions that must never happen again and the list of actions that must always happen from now on.

The forbidden actions block humanity's line of sight to God, then interrupt the message God constantly sends through nature, history, and our conscience.

Finally, the forbidden actions interfere with what God is doing on earth. The results are structures and systems not infused with divine wisdom that cannot endure.

Day 359

Replacing the name of God with any other famed name is where the madness starts. No named creature is worthy to capture and hold our attention, admiration, and trust. No named person, group or institution has ever embodied God. If a statue of a person has ever been crafted, the fame of that person is what blocks the presence of God in the society. God is the invisible Creator and does not become a visible creature to make human access and understanding easier. Why should accessing and understanding The Infinite Mind be easy? God is not a consumer product.

We remove ourselves from any human endeavor that replaces direct contact with our invisible Creator and go on to remove its lies from our minds. We unblock the flow and clear out our line of sight so we can seek God quietly, directly, daily, as close to nature as we can get. We fall silent. We don't interrupt God's message or allow other messages to interrupt and crowd out God's message to humanity.

Day 360

The earth belongs to God, including all its future creative potential. God has never authorized breaking it up into pieces, putting a price on the pieces and selling it off as a commodity. God did not create the earth as a product to be sold in a marketplace. The earth with all its massive diversity is priceless, as is any part of it. No part of it is expendable.

We turn away from any system that puts a price on creation and sells it at a profit. We remove ourselves from it as far as possible and then remove its lies from our thinking.

We turn back, seek God, and start over. We cry out to God for wisdom. We will find another way, one that does no harm to the diversity, resilience, wholeness, and beauty of God's creation. God will meet us, teach us, and help us as we figure out how to provide what we really need to grow and fulfill God's purposes.

Day 361

As part of earth, every human life belongs to God. God has never authorized breaking a life up into increments of time and selling them for a price as a commodity. We are not things to be steal, buy, or sell at a profit. No life is expendable, mere fodder to be fed into a massive, soulless deadly machine.

It is only in divinely given and guided work that we each discover what God designed us to be.

We turn away from any system that ranks people and prices them from low to high. We turn back, seek God, and start over. We cry out to God for wisdom, looking for models in nature. God will help us find another way as we figure out how to restore the dignity, meaning and joy in all necessary human labor.

Those who worship anything or anyone other than our invisible Creator will cease to exist, as will everything they built.

Those who treat the earth as property for profit will cease to exist, as will everything they built.

Those who treat human lives as property to manipulate and exploit for profit will cease to exist, as will everything they built.

Day 362

We worship our invisible Creator alone. God has no rival for our attention and admiration. We honor our Creator's purposes on earth and for earth. We treat all of creation as something wonderful, something beyond us that we must nevertheless try to understand and take care of.

We treat every human life as an undisclosed, unfolding divine mystery. We can't know the future and what God may be doing in someone's life, no matter how misguided and harmful that life may be right now.

We know God can awaken sleepwalkers, and we also know we must stay out of their way. We can hold two apparently contradictory ideas in our heads at once. Any caregiver who has endured a two-year old's tantrum learns to dislike the behavior while still believing in the child's promise.

Day 363

We dare not block, interrupt, or interfere with what God is doing in any life, and we will not allow anyone to block, interrupt, or interfere with what God is doing in our own lives. We bear the cost of these few, simple sacred values, knowing that God somehow sustains us when we do.

God has disentangled us from the complicated nonsense humans have built to enrich themselves at the expense of earth's fulness. In place of that nonsense God has deeply imprinted in us simple reasonable ways of living as part of earth, adding to its fulness.

We have internalized how God does happiness, change, diversity, and sustainability. It is not something we just study or talk about. It is more than what we do. These habituated, reflexive behaviors define who and what we are.

We are living parts in something vastly larger than ourselves individually and as a species that will outlive our species.

Day 364

Just as trees embody the divine wisdom of interdependence and cooperation, the only way God has ever been embodied on earth by humans is in the attitudes and behaviors of those who live closest to God. That is all the incarnation we ever needed or will ever need.

When our instinctive wisdom passes on to future generations through our genetics and our created works, that is all the reincarnation we ever experience or need.

Just as trees arrive at their way of living through trial and error, our likeness to God comes about over time through unlearning, re-learning, and practice until it works predictably. These lessons are encoded in us and pass on to those around us and those that follow us.

Truly, happily interconnected with God, with nature and with each other. We step across the threshold. We enter into the infinite, unfolding mystery of a sustainable future designed by God.

Day 365

Earthling, return home to earth.

Honor the will of God on earth.

Take care of what every life will need at some point.

Be courageous.

Persist in the face of setbacks and loss.

God will never abandon you.

God will come to your defense, just as you have defended God's priorities.

Nature itself, with all its vast power will come to your aid, just as you have come to the aid of nature in its hour of need.

One day it will be clear who was on God's side in this war between humanity and earth, as it becomes obvious which side has failed and which one will prevail.

Epilogue:

My daughter asked, "who is the "we" you are talking about in these books? Those who are reading these books?"

I hope so.

When two or more people...

Share the same situation

Share the same experience

Share the same sensations

Share the same feelings about their situation, experience and sensations

Share the same consistent responses

To the point that they can almost finish each other's sentences and feel less alone and more understood...

They stop thinking in terms of you and me, mine, and yours...

And start thinking in terms of us and ours...

They typically start to use the word "we" to define themselves.

If reading these books causes you to feel understood, enlivened and connected in a new way - you may belong to a new tribe, waking up and coming together across time and space.

As Heraclitus wrote:

"Those who are awake all live in the same world. Those who are asleep live their own private worlds."

Those of us who God has awakened know we live as part of one common life on earth. We recognize each other by the unique ways we constructively respond to whatever we encounter. Upon meeting each other we somehow know what to do next.

We hold God's priorities for earth in our hearts.

We hold God's unfolding future for earth in our hands.

My hope is these books might help each of us find our place in God's future, then find each other so we are less lonely and more effective.

Cordially,

Tim Daniel

"Long-lived trees make roots first."

- Ralph Waldo Emerson

www.ingramcontent.com/pod-product-compliance
Lightning Source LLC
Chambersburg PA
CBHW070609030426
42337CB00020B/3719